LEARN HOW TO

Reac
Survival Guide
to Golf

M000298467

© 2009 The Media Game, LLC
www.themediagame.com
www.GolfSurvivalGuide.com

Library of Congress Cataloging:
Ricci, Christina
Reach Your Goals Survival Guide to Golf

....

Photography by Mario Muñoz Studio, Florida
Illustrations by Robyn Neild, UK
Edited by Karen Baicker, New Jersey

REFERENCES AND QUOTES:
(pp. 33 and 34) *The Mental Game of Baseball:* A Guide to Peak Performance
Authors: H. A. Dorfman and Karl Kuehl
Publisher: Rowman & Littlefield Publishers, Inc. / January 2002

(p. 39) *Every Shot Must Have a Purpose:*
How GOLF54 Can Make You a Better Player
Authors: Pia Nilsson, Lynn Marriott, Ron Sirak
Publisher: Penguin Group (USA) / September 2005

(p. 46) Susan Choi is represented by pbmarketingagency.com,
Lynne Palazzi, President

(p. 52) Get Equipment that Fits
www.golf-club-revue.com

ISBN 978-0-9793469-0-3

Printed in China

Reach Your Goals

LEARN HOW TO TAKE YOUR GAME TO THE NEXT LEVEL

Survival Guide

YOUR goals, YOUR guide

Whether you're a casual player looking to take it up a notch, or an avid golfer trying to perfect your game, this guide offers the flexibility to reach your personal goals.

This Guide is divided into **seven sections:**

Step 1-4 » Assess Your Game

Step 1 » Self Evaluation Series Assessing your approach to the game is a critical step to reaching your goals. In this section, you will answer a series of questions that highlight why you play this game, your overall approach and mental aptitude for improvement. Honest answers will lead you to set reachable, customized goals.

Step 2 » How to Track Stats How do you know what to focus on improving if you do not have a snapshot of your current game? Explore the ways that tracking statistics can be a vital tool for improving your game.

Step 3 » Working with a Pro In this section, you will discover the importance of working with a Pro. You'll also learn how to approach your time with a Pro to maximize your lesson time as well as the time between lessons.

Step 4 » Get Equipment that Fits How old is your equipment? Do you know the best ball suited for your game? What is the loft of your putter and why do you need to know this? Learn why club fitting is a must for any player.

Step 5 » On-Course: 3 Holes This section is the core of the Guide, incorporating on-course instruction with top Pro guest appearances. I could not have achieved my first goal of dropping to a 5 handicap in 5 years without Pro-wisdom. My new goal is scratch. In order to achieve this goal, I need to focus on where I am losing the most shots out on the course and why. Follow along as we play three holes together, exploring many of the common mistakes players make out on the course including: course management decisions, common swing faults, alignment issues and much more.

Step 6 » Practice & Drills In this section, you will explore the nuts and bolts of improvement. You'll learn how to practice correctly, optimize your time at the range, on the green or at home. Be sure to check out the companion website for more tools to improve your game when off the course.

Step 7 » The Super Basics In this section, you will learn key golf etiquette, must-know rules and proper behavior so you can keep your friends and make news ones.

Look for these helpful icons along the way:

Christina's 2¢

Learn helpful tips learned and shared!

Christina's 2 Cents

Men's Tip

Women's Tip

Pro Tip

Online Video

www.golfsurvivalguide.com/reachyourgoals

Contents {COLOR CODED FOR EASY REFERENCE}

"I had no idea 10 swing thoughts, while over the ball, was a weakness in my game!"

STEP 5 » ON COURSE » 3 HOLES

Cont'd next page ☞

HOLE NUMBER TWO >> PAR 4

Cont'd next page ☞

"What the heck is he thinking about all this time? Just hit the dang ball already!"

HOLE NUMBER THREE >> PAR 3

PAR 3 >> FIRST SHOT
know your yardages AND how to focus

PERFECT YOUR CHIPS & PITCHES
learn how to hit it crisp

Cont'd next page ☞

"Don't let the chunky-monkey's mess-up your outfit!"

STEP 6 » PRACTICE & DRILLS

*"Get rid of tension...
but don't injure your
buddies!"*
Page 314

12

STEP 7 » THE SUPER BASICS

RULES & ETIQUETTE
keep your friends and make new ones

Let's begin by assessing your goals. What do you want to accomplish this season, and are these goals realistic? Early in my golfing journey, I would place unrealistic expectations on myself and come up short. I became frustrated and wondered if I was good enough to golf. But despite my shortcomings, I loved the game and wanted to continue on my journey.

I made an appointment with my Pro and asked him, "What do I need to do to reach my goal of scratch?" He asked me when I would like to achieve this goal. I said, "This year." At the time, I was an 18 handicap. The Pro assured me that yes, one day that goal would be achieved, but not this season. He explained further that to drop to scratch from an 18 in one summer is basically impossible. So... I went back to the drawing board to reevaluate my goals. My Pro helped me answer some important questions that required genuine honesty. He helped me come up with my new goal of dropping to a 12 handicap that summer. He also provided a checklist of tasks that I needed to accomplish to ensure I stayed on track So let's go ahead and evaluate your goals. It's quiz time.

On the pages that follow, you'll take two quizzes. The first focuses on reaching an honest assessment of your 'golfing' personality, motivation and approach. The second zeroes in on your on-course reactions to different scenarios, and the psychological factors affecting your game. Then you'll score your results from both quizzes and read recommendations tailored to your personal game.

In steps 2-4, you will complete your assessment by learning why tracking statistics provides critical feedback; how working with a Pro will expedite your improvement; as well as learning the best equipment for your game.

STEP 1

SELF EVALUATION SERIES

QUIZ No. 1
WHO, WHY and HOW?

We need to determine WHO you are on the course, WHY you play, and HOW you approach this wonderful game of golf. We all have a unique approach. Let's discover yours. Select the one that most applies for each question.

1. How many times do you play in a week?
- ☐ 3x+ [score: 5]
- ☐ 2x [score: 4]
- ☐ 1x [score: 3]
- ☐ less than 3x/month [score: 2]

2. Do you post your score every time you play?
- ☐ Yes [score: 5]
- ☐ No [score: 0]

3. Do you count every stroke?
- ☐ Yes [score: 5]
- ☐ No [score: 0]

4. How many mulligans do you take a round?
- ☐ Never [score: 5]
- ☐ Just 1 [score: 2]
- ☐ More than 2 [score: 0]

5. Do you track statistics?
☐ Yes [score: 5]
☐ No [score: 0]

6. How do you feel about professional lessons?
☐ I enjoy lessons and feel they are vital
   to improvement. [score: 5]
☐ Too expensive so I don't bother. [score: 2]
☐ I can learn on my own. [score: 0]

7. How many lessons do you take a month?
☐ 4 or more [score: 5]
☐ 2 [score: 4]
☐ 1 [score: 3]
☐ None [score: 0]

8. What happens after a lesson?
☐ I practice right after my lesson
   to instill the principles I just learned. [score: 5]
☐ I will practice maybe once or twice before
   my next lesson. [score: 2]
☐ I practice often between lessons. [score: 5]
☐ I play golf with my friends and I try to remember
   what my Pro said. [score: 0]

9. How into golf are you?
☐ I am obsessed and determined to get better. [score: 5]
☐ I love golf. [score: 4]
☐ I enjoy the social aspect of golf. [score: 3]
☐ It's ok. [score: 2]
☐ My spouse or parents wanted me to play. [score: 1]

10. What is your focus when scoring?
☐ I am typically thinking about the score, or the next
   hole, or about the shot I just missed. [score: 0]

Cont'd next page ☞

□ I don't keep score. [score: 1]

□ I don't count all my strokes. [score: 0]

□ I mainly focus on playing. Then I add up my score at the end. [score: 5]

11. Do you like to practice?

□ I enjoy practicing at the range. [score: 4]

□ I enjoy practicing on the course. [score: 4]

□ I enjoy practicing at the range and on-course. [score: 5]

□ It's ok. [score: 3]

□ I hate to practice. [score: 0]

12. How often do you practice?

□ 3x+ /week [score: 5]

□ 2x /week [score: 4]

□ 1x /week [score: 2]

□ Less than 1x /week [score: 1]

□ Never [score: 0]

13. What do you practice?

□ Mostly long game [score: 1]

□ Long game and chipping [score: 3]

□ Long game, chipping, putting [score: 4]

□ Long game, chipping, putting, wedge shots [score: 5]

□ Never [score: 0]

14. How long do you practice each session?

□ 2 or more hours [score: 5]

□ 1 hour [score: 4]

□ 1/2 hour [score: 3]

□ Never [score: 0]

15. Do you know any drills?

□ Yes [score: 5]

□ No [score: 0]

16. Do you practice any drills?
- ☐ Yes [score: 5]
- ☐ No [score: 0]

17. Do you practice at home?
- ☐ Huh? [score: 0]
- ☐ I love to work in front of the mirror on my posture or backswing. [score: 4]
- ☐ I work on my putting. [score: 4]
- ☐ I work on my putting and mirror work. [score: 5]

18. Which best describes your style of practice at the range?
- ☐ I hit 2 or more buckets and spend 1/2 hour or less around the green or putting. [score: 3]
- ☐ I hit 2 or more buckets, and I spend at least an hour on short game. [score: 5]
- ☐ I hit 1 bucket, no short game. [score: 2]
- ☐ I hit 1 bucket and spend a 1/2 hour or less on short game. [score: 3]
- ☐ I hit 1 bucket, and spend an hour or more on short game. [score: 5]

19. What is your pre-shot routine?
- ☐ I have no idea what that is. [score: 0]
- ☐ I do not have one. [score: 1]
- ☐ A specific routine I do with my driver. [score: 2]
- ☐ A specific routine I do with every shot including on the green. [score: 5]

20. How strong is your confidence?
- ☐ I lose confidence after one bad shot. [score: 0]
- ☐ I lose confidence after five bad shots. [score: 2]
- ☐ Bad shots don't affect me. I go to the range and work it out. [score: 5]

Cont'd next page ☞

21. How many thoughts do you have during a swing?

☐ I have only one. [score: 5]

☐ I have two. [score: 4]

☐ I can't count that high. [score: 0]

☐ None except, what is my target? [score: 5]

22. What is your typical percentage of focus on every shot during an 18 hole round?

☐ 100% on every shot during the round. [score: 5]

☐ 100% on roughly 12 of 18 holes. [score: 3]

☐ 50% on every shot for 9 holes. I lose focus on the back 9. [score: 2]

☐ Sporadic, if I am in the woods or in a bunker. [score: 1]

23. What happens at the range?

☐ I just go and hit balls. [score: 1]

☐ I just go hit balls, and then spend a few minutes before I leave putting a few. [score: 2]

☐ I just hit balls, but I work on things from my lesson. [score: 4]

☐ I hit balls working on a specific task, such as, alignment. Then I will work on a specific putting drill or chipping technique. [score: 5]

24. What is the fastest road to improvement as you see it?

☐ I will try any training aid, a quick tip or fix, looking for the secret of the golf swing. I know it's out there. [score: 0]

☐ The fastest road to improvement is quantity. The more I hit balls at the range, the better I will get. [score: 1]

☐ I believe only practice is the way to go. In fact, I prefer to practice than play. [score: 2]

☐ I believe a balanced mixture of lessons, practice and on-course playing is the fastest road to improvement. [score: 5]

25. What is your typical mental state before you hit a shot?

☐ I feel a sense of fear or nervousness. [score: 3]

☐ I feel a sense of confidence. [score: 5]

☐ I think to myself, "I have no idea where this ball is going." [score: 0]

☐ I am still thinking about the last shot I just played. [score: 0]

Add up your score and write it here

Overall Approach Quiz 1 Score

· ·
                                          ⋮
                                          ▼

_____

MENTAL TOUGHNESS

QUIZ No. 2

HOW do you react?

You just shanked a 50-yard wedge into the back of the bunker. You are now left with a downhill lie to a tight pin. You proceed to skull the shot and walk away with a nine. Do you beat yourself up for the next three holes, or does it roll right off you? How you react to on-course situations affects your aptitude for improvement and overall success. Are you more positive or negative in your thinking and behavioral patterns? Take this quiz to determine your reactional behavioral patterns. Select the one that most describes what you would do in the following situations.

ACCOUNTABILITY

Scenario A:

You were playing great for 9 holes, your record best. Then, all of a sudden; your ball is spraying left, you are duffing your chips and the round is going down the toilet. You:

- ☐ Call yourself names like, "You are a loser." [score: 0]
- ☐ Resolve you are heading to the range after this round. [score: 5]
- ☐ Start throwing clubs. [score: 0]
- ☐ Accept it, it's a beautiful day. [score: 5]
- ☐ Blame it on the wind, or slow greens. [score: 2]
- ☐ Worry that your friends will not want to play with you after this awful round. [score: 1]

☐ Refocus on staying in the present and hitting your best shot. [score: 5]

Scenario B:
You are around the green for an easy up and down for Par, but the last time you chunked your shot and got a triple from 40 yards. You:

☐ Fear that you will choke and chunk the shot, just like you did before. [score: 0]

☐ Are excited to make this shot a success. [score: 4]

☐ Feel confident because you worked on this at the range; the other day is a distant memory. [score: 5]

Scenario C:
You have 3-putted every green. You think it is because of:

☐ Your yapping buddies. [score: 1]

☐ Your putts; they were just missing the cup. [score: 5]

☐ Your putter; you are buying a new one. [score: 0]

☐ You. You're a horrible putter anyway, so no surprise. [score: 0]

CONFIDENCE

Scenario A:
You are faced with a shot you have never tried. You:

☐ Fear that you will choke. [score: 1]

☐ Get excited to attempt this shot. [score: 5]

☐ Get upset and think, "I always get the bad shots!" [score: 0]

☐ Give it your all and hope for the best. [score: 5]

Cont'd next page

23

Scenario B:

You are playing in a tournament and if you sink this putt you and your partner win. You:

- ☐ Begin to sweat and shake over the putt. All you can think about is, "Don't miss this putt!" [score: 0]
- ☐ Putt the same way you have been; choose the line and trust it. [score: 5]
- ☐ Think about what your partner will say if you miss. [score: 1]

Scenario C:

You are faced with a shot that needs to carry over a bunker to a tight pin. You:

- ☐ Choke and skull the shot over the green. [score: 0]
- ☐ Are excited to try that flop shot that you read about in a golf magazine. [score: 5]

EXPECTATIONS

Scenario A:

On the 16th hole you realize you are two strokes away from breaking your current record score. You tee it up, visualizing shooting that record number, but instead you get a triple bogey on 17 and double bogey 18. You:

- ☐ Talk to yourself. "I'll never break 90." [score: 0]
- ☐ On the 18th after you 3-putt, louisville-slugger your ball in the water in disgust. [score: 0]
- ☐ Get depressed; the day is ruined. [score: 0]
- ☐ Accept it. You will do better tomorrow. [score: 5]

☐ Blame it on your yapping friends. [score: 1]

☐ Worry your friends will think you suck. [score: 1]

☐ Call your Pro, time for a lesson. [score: 4]

Scenario B:

You just won the Club Championship.

☐ You are pleased because you played your best. [score: 5]

☐ You are hoping your success gets the praise from the Club Pro. [score: 2]

☐ You are hoping your rival or buddies at the club hear about this. [score: 3]

Scenario C:

You attempted a really tough shot that you have not practiced:

☐ You give it your best but don't have any expectations. After all, you have not practiced this shot much. [score: 5]

☐ Focus on a similar set-up from another shot. [score: 5]

☐ Slam your club after a poor execution. [score: 0]

CHOKE-FACTOR

Scenario A:

You are on the tee box teeing it up and your buddies are getting off 9. They wait to watch you tee off and say hi. You:

☐ Feel self-conscious and proceed to top the ball twenty feet in front of you. [score: 1]

☐ Love the audience and proceed to rip it down the fairway. [score: 4]

☐ Friends? I didn't even know they were there. [score: 5]

Cont'd next page ☞

☐ Hit the ball in the woods and proceed to blame it on your friends for distracting you. [score: 0]

Scenario B:

You have a fried egg in the bunker to a tight pin and water just beyond. You're betting with your friends and your team is two down. Over the shot you are thinking;

☐ "Don't go in the water!" [score: 0]

☐ "Oh dear God, please let me get this out!" [score: 2]

☐ "Ok, focus on set-up and stay in the shot." [score: 5]

Scenario C:

The course is backed up, and there are two groups on the tee. You are up. You:

☐ Think to yourself, "Please don't go in the woods." [score: 0]

☐ Do your normal routine. [score: 5]

☐ Get nervous and swing a bit faster than normal. [score: 2]

TRUST

Scenario A:

How do you recover if the previous shot was not a success?

☐ You choke and skull the shot over the green. [score: 0]

☐ You focus more, but just to get the hole over. [score: 3]

☐ You focus more, up for the challenge. [score: 5]

☐ You don't care anymore. [score: 2]

Scenario B:

You are up on the tee box and you notice the lake running alongside the entire left side of the fairway. You say to yourself:

- ☐ "Don't go in the water." [score: 0]
- ☐ "I am going for the 150 yard stake." [score: 5]
- ☐ "If I miss, where do I want to miss to avoid the trouble?" [score: 5]
- ☐ "Ok, make a big shoulder turn, use your legs," or other mechanical-oriented thoughts. [score: 0]

Cont'd next page ☞

Scenario C:

You are over a double breaking downhill, down grain putt. You:

☐ Adjust your putterface at the last moment. [score: 0]

☐ Analyze every angle, but still doubt the line. [score: 2]

☐ Trust your first read and focus on speed. [score: 5]

ATTITUDE

Scenario A:

You had a rough day at the office; in fact, this whole week has been a nightmare… and now you just 3-putted. You:

☐ Throw your ball in the lake. [score: 0]

☐ Start swearing and saying things like, "I suck at this game!" [score: 0]

☐ Chuckle, and think "Well, at least I am out of the office." [score: 5]

☐ Blame your miss on your 'stinking' putter. [score: 0]

Scenario B:

The 'Golf Gods' are not with you today. You are not scoring and have not hit one solid shot all day. You are only on 11. You:

☐ Feel a sense of anxiety stirring. [score: 2]

☐ Quicken your tempo and your swing gets worse. [score: 1]

☐ Make more negative comments with each shot. [score: 0]

☐ Decide it's just one of those days, and tomorrow will be better. [score: 5]

☐ Regroup and take deep breaths, because you know if you relax and focus, your game has a chance. [score: 5]

Scenario C:

You finished the round of your life. After the round, you:

☐ Celebrate with your friends. [score: 5]

☐ Are pleased but think you could have played
a few holes better to shoot even lower. [score: 4]

☐ Are hoping your rival or buddies at the club hear
about this. [score: 2]

Add up your score for each category and write it here.

Mental Toughness Quiz 2 Score

Accountability ....➤ _____

Confidence ....➤ _____

Expectations ....➤ _____

Choke-Factor..➤ _____

Trust ....➤ _____

Attitude ....➤ _____

SCORE RESULTS QUIZ 1
Who, Why and How you approach your game

Our goal is to determine what you can expect in your improvement process based on the answers to QUIZ No 1. By establishing realistic expectations based on your overall approach on the course and at the range, we can hone in on achievable goals.

Answers to Quiz No. 1:

Add up your score and read what you can expect on your road to better golf this season.

If you scored 105 or higher

You are on the fast track to serious improvement. You have good practice habits and can put in the time to drop your handicap considerably this season. However, let's ensure your goals are realistic, narrow your focus, and assess exactly where you are losing the most strokes. With a clear snapshot of your game, establish a plan of action to focus on your weak areas and make them your strengths. Lastly, let's develop stronger practice habits both on and off the course.

If you scored 80-104

You can realistically drop up to 5 strokes off your handicap this season. You spend some time at the range, take lessons, though maybe not as much as you like. With slight to moderate readjustment at the range and on the course, you can see improvement. Let's determine one key area to focus on before we proceed to the next area for improvement. This will allow for a targeted approach that will yield better scores and more enjoyment with your game. Keep in mind: the lower your current handicap, the slower the drop.

If you scored 0-79

You can realistically drop 1-2 strokes off your handicap this season. You spend little time at the range; perhaps lessons are not in the budget or on the agenda. If you are interested in improving this season, you can. Pay special attention to *Step 5 - On Course*. In addition, let's get you practicing more, but correctly. If time is an issue—kids, or your job—try at home drills so you can improve this season.

Good news for all

Your score does not reflect the entire picture. As long as you have an interest in improving and are willing to dedicate what you can to that endeavor, then you will see improvement. The first step is to learn where you are losing the most strokes and addressing your strengths and weaknesses out on the course from tee to green. By understanding which of these components affect your shot-making ability, you can make a plan of action. Second, let's learn good practice, budget a series of lessons, and work on a few drills that address those weak areas of your game.

However, understand that the more you commit and dedicate to a plan, the faster the results. Awareness is one thing, but actively committing is another. This is not a casual endeavor, but it can certainly be fun, enlightening and enjoyable because you are making a statement to yourself, facing your inner demons, and saying "ENOUGH IS ENOUGH!" Requirements for improvement are patience, a strong will (no wishy-washiness) and perseverance. Our goal is to REPLACE bad habits with good habits. So let's get started…

SCORE RESULTS
FOR QUIZ 2
HOW you react

Christina's 2¢

You have the power to change. All you need is the will and a wee bit of time!

You need to improve an area if you received less than a 10 on any of the topics from the quiz, but keep in mind: what is presented here is just a starting point. The good news: **you can** improve the six inches between your ears. I did. I have struggled with every topic presented ten-fold, so I have shared a few of my own journeys.

ACCOUNTABILITY

You need to work on **taking responsibility for your actions** and not allow excuses to control you. Take a moment to recount your self-talk after a poorly executed shot. Was it something like: "I hate these greens today," or "The pace of play is too slow. I am losing my focus."or, blaming a missed shot because of your yapping buddies while you were over a putt? All these reasons why you missed the shot may have a ring of truth; however, blaming these conditions will not improve the outcome of that shot or your next shot.

You and only you have control over your thoughts and actions. You have a choice to think either positive or negative thoughts. I know you may be thinking, "Sometimes these thoughts just pop-in almost like they come out of nowhere." A good method that will change your shot process is learning how to focus. Focus on your game, not external factors. Give one hundred percent with each shot—this leaves no room for misguided focus such as distractive and shot-sabotaging excuses. Committing to a routine and staying in the moment will give you the best opportunity for a successful outcome.

The next time you are playing be aware of what you are thinking. If your thoughts are self-sabotaging or dripping with negative language, change to more positive thoughts such as, "I love my putting." or, "I am going for it this time."

"Remember this: one of the strongest principles of behavior lies in human choice. If you do not take responsibility, you have still made a choice. A wrong one."

    - H.A. Dorfman and Karl Kuehl, *The Mental Game of Baseball*

CONFIDENCE

The number one question I get asked from players, "How do I find confidence when I have lost it after a few bad shots?" If you struggle with confidence, ask yourself why. Is it because you feel you cannot execute a shot? Is it because your swing is temporarily lost? Or, is it because you are new to the game and you are worried what others will think of you? The **courage to face obstacles** is required in most endeavors, from sports to the game of life. You can develop confidence by paralleling past successes with preparation for future attempts. For example, the more you practice a particular shot or technique, the more confident you become to perform the same shot again on the course.

When you are facing a shot you have never attempted, you have a choice: stand up to the challenge with enthusiasm; get creative with the shot; or become paralyzed with fear or self-doubt, and mentally quit—pouting, "I can't do this."

Our goal is to build our confidence level so that when faced with new challenges, we will face them with courage and commitment. How do we achieve this? Knowledge—knowledge is power. Build a library of knowledge to draw on for any situation you encounter on the course. Even if you did not successfully execute a shot, you can walk away with a smile knowing you gave the shot your full attention—a one hundred percent commitment with fortitude.

There will be many shots you are unsure of your ability to execute, but your reserve of confidence will provide the courage you need to give it your best shot. You will never make that birdie putt if you do not get the ball past the hole. Success is defined not by the outcome, but by the process—the journey.

"Yes, we know rationally what it takes to succeed, but our emotions interfere with that understanding when we're faced by a challenge we do not think we're up to. So we have to recognize the emotions that are inhibiting our bodies and control them with winning mind games—strong, positive thoughts focused on function."

- H.A. Dorfman and Karl Kuehl, *The Mental Game of Baseball*

EXPECTATIONS

If you ask five golfers what their expectations are on the course, you will get five different answers. Expectations are **what we believe we can achieve**. Everyone's expectations are different. Yes, we all want to play good golf, but to what end? Your expectations need to mirror your willingness and diligence to achieve the desired outcome—what you expect your efforts can produce.

I have always set high expectations for myself on and off the course. I am driven by a bombardment of goals that I feel must be met yesterday. As you can imagine, this mindset leads to frustration, disappointment, and sometimes anger. On the other hand, when I do meet my goals I am elated and encouraged to forge ahead at warp speed. However, golf has taught me that warp speed is not necessarily a good thing. The learning process requires a focused commitment, a positive attitude, and, above all, patience.

Lastly, the goals you set must be yours and yours alone. They should never be driven by your coach, impressing your buddies, or seeking the approval from others. They do not define you—only you have that power. Once we let others dictate our goals and expectations, we lose control of the one thing we need to achieve success—joy for the game. Without joy, improvement is worthless.

"All power is from within and therefore, under our control."
- Robert Collier

CHOKE-FACTOR

One of the biggest lessons for me was discovering that my tension levels were through the roof! I discovered the main culprit was my own high expectations and seeking approval from others. I failed to produce my desired outcome when the eyes of others were upon me. I discovered the driving emotion behind these failures was fear—**fear of 'choking'**. Fear is the number one cause of tension. Tension is the 'numero-uno' cause of bad swings.

Ask yourself, "What is the worst that could happen? I miss the shot—big deal." You may be thinking, "Yes, I missed the shot and now I am really embarrassed in front of my peers." Trust me, they will not remember that shot tomorrow. Another culprit that triggers the 'choke-factor' is unrealistic expectations, setting yourself up for failure before you step on the first tee box. The most unproductive instigator of fear is negative self-questioning, such as:

"What if this goes in the water?"

"What if I miss this putt?"

"What will my friends think of me if I shoot over 100?"

If I could go back to day one, I would not have one ounce of tension in my body. There is a tremendous difference in a swing with tension and a swing that is tension-free. Loose muscles are faster than tight muscles. Tension is an issue we all face. It affects everything from shot success to mental stamina.

The easiest way to eliminate fear is staying in the moment and *accepting* your game at this moment. Staying in the moment allows you to be absorbed in the task at hand such as set-up, good tempo, and target. This leaves no room for worrying about the outcome, which ultimately, produces the dreaded 'choke-factor'.

TRUST

In my early days, I wish I focused more on **believing in my own abilities** than worrying about mechanics. I would get to the tee box and the thoughts rolled in like a fierce storm; "Ok, make a full shoulder turn, use your legs in the downswing," and the list went on. Instead, I should have been focusing on my target. The problem: I did not trust my ability to make a swing. I would practice four to five days a week. I certainly visited my Pro on a regular basis, so why didn't I trust my body to swing the club?

Another scenario: how many times have you stood on the tee box thinking, "I hope I do not hit the ball in the water." You tee off and miraculously the ball goes into the water. Why did this happen? The subconscious mind cannot distinguish between *do* and *don't*. It simply goes where your thoughts and energies go. Think of it as a self-fulfilling prophecy.

Another scenario: how often do you read a putt, trust your first instinct, and the putt goes in? Conversely, you see the line and then you proceed to analyze the line from every angle, like *Tiger*, thinking that if you do not analyze from every angle you will miss the putt. It takes about five seconds to feel the line—our brains and body are smart—give them credit and trust your instincts. When I am over a putt and I am misaligned, my body feels awkward. I feel a bit of tension creep in out of nowhere. When this happens, I step back and realign.

Do you think about how to walk when you are walking? Or what about when you are driving in heavy traffic and you are late for an appointment. You weave in and out of traffic like *Mario Andretti* without a second thought. So let's all ask ourselves, "Why do we overthink everything in golf?" It's really quite astounding. The bottom line: learn to trust your inner voice and inner body sensations when you are out on the course—you will begin to see dramatic improvement.

So how did I learn to trust my body to swing the club? By letting go of expectations, trusting my inner voice, and accepting my game at this moment. It is quite exhilarating for me because I struggled with trust for most of my golfing journey. Now when I swing the club, I feel a sense of freedom. There is no effort, no 'trying' to hit it far, nor 'trying' to do this or that through impact. I simply turn and fire to my finish—what happens in between is usually pretty good. I am letting my hard work on the range pay off without interference from me.

ATTITUDE

Attitude is, by far, the biggest lesson golf has taught me. I am very competitive by nature—a Type A, a high achiever. My expectations are very high of myself and others. This sometimes works to my benefit. Other times, it just gets in my way.

My search for perfection nearly ended my golfing journey. I spent hours at the range, thousands of dollars for lessons, but did not see improvement. I was stuck in the high 80's, early 90's. My goal was to be a scratch player, so you can imagine my frustration. "Why was I wasting my time on this game?" I had been playing for four years and felt like giving up.

My nature is never to give up, so I ventured off to *54 Golf's* 3-day golf school, where I discovered just how bad my **lack of composure and dignity** was towards the process of learning. I was too negative. Every bad shot I would huff and puff or slam my club. I would get so angry that it would ruin my day and everyone else's around me. Sometimes, I would leave the course in tears. What I learned was, anger makes us stupid, literally. Our brains release a chemical that clouds our judgment, our focus, zaps our energy, and most importantly eliminates our joy. My joy for the game was lost, but my hope in recovering it was still alive.

Once I realized this, I redirected my focus to address my reactions to bad shots. I accepted them, and shifted my focus from mechanics to actually playing the game of golf. My scores began to drop. I didn't need to spend more time practicing or shelling out more money for lessons. I had the swing; it was trapped inside my idea of where I thought my game should be. Literally, four months after returning from *54 Golf*, my handicap dropped from an eight to a five! I was thrilled! My joy of the game was rediscovered.

Christina's 2¢

Accept your game and embrace it!

I realized, and this took me another few years, that the most important lesson golf taught me was to accept where I am at this moment. My advice: accept your game and embrace it. Yes, strive to be better, but at the end of the day, it is the company you keep during those four hours and eighteen holes that matter the most. They will not remember your score, but they will remember your attitude.

"Find something good to say about every shot you hit–or say nothing at all."
- Pia Nilsson and Lynn Marriott,
Every Shot Must Have A Purpose

The Bottom Line: PLAYING IN "A" MOMENT

We've all heard of **staying in the present**. Play one shot at a time. Sounds easy enough—just hit the damn shot, right? Yeah right. It requires an understanding of all these six components rolled into one moment. Here is a checklist to ensure you stay in the moment:

• Are your **expectations** and goals in check?
• Do you **trust** your ability to execute this shot without **fear of choking**—with full **confidence**, commitment and focus?

• Do you accept full **accountability** for every shot and its outcome?
• Do you have a positive **attitude** towards learning, and your game **at this moment**?

By understanding which of these components affect your shot-making ability, you can now make a plan of action. However, understand that the more you commit to a plan the better and faster the results. Awareness is one thing, but actively committing

"Accept your game at this moment."

is another. This is not a casual endeavor, but it can certainly be fun. You are standing up to yourself, facing your inner demons, saying, "ENOUGH IS ENOUGH, let's focus on improving the right way!"

Recommended reading:

» "Golf, The Ultimate Mind Game" by Rick Sessinghaus
» "The Inner Game of Golf" by W. Timothy Gallwey
» "Zen Golf: Mastering the Mental Game" by Joseph Parent
» "Harvey Penick's Little Red Book: Lessons and Teachings from a Lifetime in Golf" by Harvey Penick
» "Golf is Not a Game of Perfect" by Dr. Bob Rotella
» "The Mental Game of Baseball: A Guide to Peak Performance" by H A Dorfman and Karl Kuehl
» "Fearless Golf: Conquering the Mental Game" by Dr. Gio Valiante
» "Every Shot Must Have a Purpose" by Pia Nilsson and Lynn Marriott

What are YOUR GOALS?

Ok, now you know what you can expect this season based on the answers to the series of questions from Quiz 1 and 2. When defining your GOALS, be sure to take these points into consideration: if you scored a 40 on the quiz and you are a 22 handicap, please do not expect to drop to a 10 handicap by the end of the season. However, if you are able to make the necessary changes to score higher on the quiz, which is very doable, then reassess after one month. Retake the Evaluation Series and reassess your goals.

First, download a Goal Assesment worksheet. Here you will establish five goals for this season. When writing your goals, keep in mind, **goals need to be measurable**, so it is best to set numerical goals with a time-frame. You will refer to these goals every time you play or practice. I suggest posting these goals in your car, by your nightstand, or on your bathroom mirror for those overachievers.

Before you can complete your goal assessment worksheet, you first need to track your statistics for the next five rounds. Learn how and what to track on the next pages. Tracking stats will give you a starting point so you can begin to identify where you are losing shots.

With measurable goals established based on realistic and inner-targeted expectations, let's see what we can do to help you reach those goals. Remember, our mission is to get you playing your best golf on a consistent basis. This includes learning how to focus better at the practice range AND out on the course.

Download a Goal Assessment Worksheet. A guy and girl's version is available. Download at: www.golfsurvivalguide.com/reachyourgoals

My Goal Assessment

Today's Date

What I need to work on this year to break _____!

5 Goals for this season:

_____

_____

_____

_____

	Current	Goal
Fairways Hit		
GIRs		
Putts per round		
Average score		
Number of doubles		
Number of bogeys		
Number of pars		
Number of birdies		

Based on 5 rounds

Girl's version shown here

Examples:

Goal 1: I would like to average under 34 putts by the end of the summer.

Goal 2: I would like 10 more yards off the tee by the end of this season.

	1	2	3	4	5	6	7	8	9	OUT
71.8/132	386	352	173	519	416	199	538	192	421	319
70.2/124	369	331	160	496	395	182	488	170	402	293
M: 68.5/122	349	317	140	477	372	165	473	150	383	285
W: 73.4/130										
	11	13	17	1	7	15	5	9	3	
ap	11	13	17	1	7	5	4	7	3	
Christina	3	4	3	6	5	/	1	/	/	
Fairways	1	0	/	1	0	0	0	1	1	
GIR's	1	1	1	1	0	0	0	1	1	
Putts	1	1	2	2	2	2	3	2		
		1	1	2	2	2	2	3	2	
		4	4	3	5	4	3	5	3	4
Par										

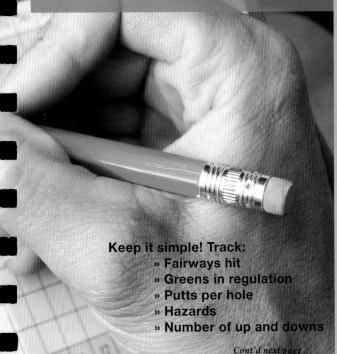

HOW CAN YOU IMPROVE IF YOU HAVE NO IDEA WHERE YOU NEED THE IMPROVEMENT?

An easy way to establish a starting point and to monitor progress is by tracking your statistics. Begin by tracking fairways hit, greens in regulation, and number of putts per round every time you play. You will begin to see the error of your ways. Once you have at least 5 rounds of statistics, take these to your Pro for evaluation.

Keep it simple! Track:
 » **Fairways hit**
 » **Greens in regulation**
 » **Putts per hole**
 » **Hazards**
 » **Number of up and downs**

Cont'd next page

How to determine your **weaknesses,** and **overcome them.**

{ **By Susan Choi,** *LPGA Duramed Futures Tour Player and Competitor on The Big Break Ka'anapali*

Keeping your statistics in a golf journal is a great way of discovering your strengths and weaknesses. When you play a round of golf, keep track of how many fairways you hit, how many greens in regulations you hit, and total number of putts per hole and per round. I even keep stats on scrambling (up and down if I miss a green) and sandys (if I get up and down from the bunker).

If you keep track of your statistics in a journal, then you will be able to pinpoint where you lose strokes in most of your rounds. For example, if you three putt frequently, you should work on your putting (lag putts, short putts).

First you need to find out where you lose most of your shots. Then work from there. You want to make your weaknesses your strengths. For me, my strength is my short game. When I first started playing golf, I struggled out of the bunker. I worked very diligently on making that my strength... now I love the bunker!

	1	2	3	4	5	6	7	8	9
PAR	4	5	3	4	5	4	3	4	4
SCORE	4	6	3	5	7	4	2	4	5
PUTTS	2	2	2	2	3	2	1	2	2
PENALTY					X				

	10	11	12	13	14	15	16	17	18
PAR									
SCORE									
PUTTS									
PENALTY									

O 2 | 3| 4 5 6 7 8 9 10 11 12 13 14 15 16 17 18
O = Fairways Hit / = Par 3

O 2 O 4 5 6 7 8 9 10 11 12 13 14 15 16 17 18
Greens in Regulation

Out: _____ In: _____ Total: _____

1 Putts _____ 2 Putts _____ 3 Putts _____ Total _____ Average _____

Eagles _____ Birdies _____ Par _____ Bogeys _____ Dbl Bogeys _____ Other _____

Over/Under: _____
Par 3 _____ Par 4 _____ Par 5 _____ Penalty _____

COURSE: Key Biscayne
Date: 1/23/09   Time of Play: 11am
Conditions: Windy and Sunny
6425   792   140
Course Yardage   Course Rating   Slope Rating
Holes Played: 18   Par: 72   Tee Box: Whites
Name/Score: Christina Ricci
Name/Score:
Name/Score:
Notes: I need to pu

Architect: _____   Built: _____

GET A SURVIVAL GUIDE STATS JOURNAL!

If you are new to stats, begin tracking stats on your scorecard or even better, get a *Survival Guide Stats Journal*. You can also enter your statistics online. I use an online program called *Scorecard* to create graphs and other cool statistical data.

Christina's 2¢

Get an honest assessment of your game with stats.

A WISE INVESTMENT IF IMPROVEMENT IS ON YOUR AGENDA

If you are serious about improving your game this season, I highly suggest you invest time and a few dollars with a local Pro. The key is to find a Pro who suits your game. If your wallet is tight, organize a group lesson and share the costs. Most clubs offer clinics for a reasonable fee. This is a great way to check out the Pro to see if there is a fit. To find a Pro in your area, visit PGA.com or LPGA.com.

Maximize Your Lesson-time

I could not have reached my first goal of becoming a 5 handicap in 5 years from a 30 without a professional golf instructor. I visit my Pro about once a month to make sure my set-up and alignment are in check. In the early days, I would schedule two or three lessons a month because I was determined to be the best player I could be in the least amount of time. Single digits was my goal, so I knew the effort it would require to achieve this goal.

Christina's 2¢

Stay on track with your game plan. If you deviate…3 steps back!

The key to a successful relationship with a Pro is to stick to the plan. If you have a lesson, but then in between, do not practice on the principles from the lesson, or discover some short-cut tip you read in a magazine, you will lose focus and take three steps back instead of three steps ahead.

Another equally important lesson I discovered is that the learning process is slow. I like things done yesterday and what I discovered about golf, you cannot rush the learning process. I tried to absorb too much information during my lessons—no good. It is best to work on ONE thing and keep with it until you get it. Then you can add to that, like building a house. You need to lay the foundation first before you can add the roof.

Lastly, find a Pro who suits your learning style. I am a visual learner, so I like lessons where I can see my swing on the big screen and analyze what's going on. What you feel and what's real are two different things entirely. So for me, an instructor who had these tools worked best for me. Find a Pro who suits your needs and you will reach your goals much faster, in 'golf time' that is, not lightning speed!

If a Pro is not in your budget, go for the clinics or a group lesson where you share the cost. This is also a great way to check out various Pros with different teaching styles to learn who will fit your needs.

Monthly visits with my Pro are like tune-ups, keeping my form in check.

STEP 4

GET EQUIPMENT

THAT FITS

Clubs that Fit

How the golf club fitting variables affect your game

You wouldn't borrow your friend's hand-me-down bras would you? So why would you use your friend's hand-me-down clubs or your husband's set of clubs that have been sitting in the garage since the 40's? Or guys who are 6'4", you wouldn't use standard length shafts would you? Club fitting in the early days was considered only worthy of professional golfers. Today, club fitting is a highly recommended endeavor, whether you are a beginner with ten rounds or an avid golfer with a thousand rounds.

What Is 'Golf Club Fitting'?

Club fitting is adjusting clubs to your individual swing speed, height, arm length, hand size, swing shape and swing tempo. A good fitting measures all these parameters and then adjusts your clubs accordingly. Clubs can be adjusted for length, lie, shaft flex, shaft bend point, grip size, and swing weight.

Club fitting also means helping you choose clubheads with the right forgiveness and ball flight characteristics to fit your particular abilities. The correct adjustments will make a club easier to hit and maximize distance for you.

You can also select clubs that address a particular weakness in your game. Most golfers' games usually need one of three things—more consistency, distance or accuracy. Sometimes they

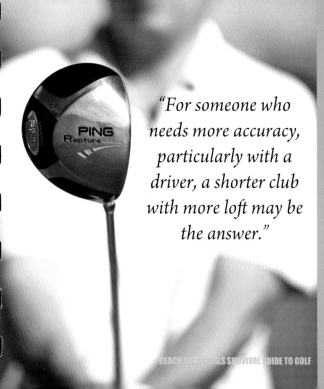

"For someone who needs more accuracy, particularly with a driver, a shorter club with more loft may be the answer."

need all three. Your golf clubs can be adjusted to help in any or all of these areas.

If you are a beginner or someone who plays very seldom, consistency may be an issue for you. Your lack of playing time makes center of clubface contact a little harder to maintain. Choosing clubheads that offer maximum forgiveness can really help you. Features like perimeter weighting, offset hosels, oversizing, low-back center of gravity and wide soles can mean a clubhead that has a larger sweetspot, higher ball flight and less of a tendency to twist on mishits. It can all add up to straighter, higher shots and more forgiveness.

For someone who needs more accuracy, particularly with a driver, a shorter club with more loft may be the answer. More loft creates more back spin, which means the side spin that causes the ball to curve will be less of a factor. The shorter length will help create more center-of-the-club-face contact, which will also make the ball go straighter—and as a side benefit, a bit farther.

If what you really require is more distance, then shaft flex, swing weight and driver loft become important. For example: Suppose your club head speed is between 80-90 mph—close to the average for most male golfers and better female golfers. For that swing speed your driver should hit the ball about 200 yards in the air. The best shaft flex for that speed would be a regular flex shaft. However tests have proven that getting the ball to stay in the air as long as possible creates the most distance. The ideal launch angle to make that happen would be about 13 degrees. That translates to a driver loft of about 11 or 12 degrees. The result would be about 5 or 6 yards of additional carry distance.

It's even more important for slower swing speeds. For a club head speed of 60-70 mph, typical of seniors, women and juniors, the potential carry distance is around 150 yards. The correct launch angle is more like 18 degrees. So a driver loft of 13-15 degrees is optimal. This can increase distance as much as 15 yards for these swing speeds—a big difference.

Steel versus Graphite

What's the deal?

The benefit of graphite shafts is they are lighter, so you can swing them faster. Graphite is a good idea for any of the distance clubs—drivers, woods, and long hybrids. Graphite is also a good idea if you have a slow swing speed. Graphite also offers a softer feel and less contact vibration. Steel shafts are better for faster swing speeds and for the accuracy clubs such as irons and particularly wedges.

DOES IT MATTER WHAT TYPE OF BALL I USE?

YES!

Under the Rules of Golf, a golf ball can weigh no more than 1.620 oz (45.93 grams), have a diameter not less than 1.680 in (42.67 mm), and must perform within specified velocity, distance, and symmetry limits.

A **Ball** that Fits

What is the best golf ball for you based on your game, playing needs and goals? And of course, don't forget about your budget. Golf balls have become quite expensive in the higher end of the scale. Choosing the right golf ball can help your game and save you money.

Of course you are getting quite a bit more for your money.

Compared to 20 years ago, today's top-of-the-line balls are great—assuming you can keep from losing them. You certainly won't have to worry about cutting them up like the old balata balls.

The big question is 'are they worth it' for your game?

Golf ball selection is worth some serious thought because the golf balls on the lower end of the cost scale have gotten quite a bit better too. Even you low handicappers can get great balls for your game—if you don't let your pride get in the way. Here's what you need to know to make that decision.

GENERAL GOLF BALL TYPES

Distance Balls A ball designed to react quickly off the clubface for maximum speed which results in overall distance. Distance balls are often two-piece designs with cores designed for maximum velocity off the clubface.

Spin Control A ball designed to reduce spin and help manage hook or slice tendencies. Golfers who are seeking to reduce hooks and slices may seek a low-spin golf ball. These are generally two-piece balls with specially designed covers.

Total Performance A ball intended to create the best balance of spin, distance and control. Total performance balls are often multi-layer, multi-construction golf balls. Total performance balls are preferred by better players. These can be 3- or 4-piece balls.

GOLF BALL CONSTRUCTION

Two-Piece Balls feature dual construction made up of a large solid inner core (that generates excellent distance) surrounded by a high restitution outer cover. This enables maximum energy transfer to the ball at impact.

Multi-Layer Balls are typically three or four layers in which the core is wrapped in one or two mantle layers under an outer cover. Three-piece and four-piece golf balls are a good match for golfers with moderate to high clubhead speeds who want distance and feel.

THE 2-PIECE BALL: Best for Beginners and Intermediate Players
A two-piece ball is usually the least expensive. This construction is used by 60 to 70 percent of golfers. The core is typically synthetic rubber that's been heated and pressurized to harden it, which gives the ball lots of speed. The cover is generally made of ionomer, a type of plastic, and is often thicker than the covers on three-piece or four-piece balls. As a result, they tend to be more durable. The balls tend to be harder, so they spin less.

THE 3-PIECE BALL: Best for More Experienced Players
Provides low spin off a driver to go far, yet provides more spin off iron shots, for better golfers who can, for instance, create backspin that causes the ball to roll less after it lands on the green. May cost twice as much as a two-piece. The core is typically synthetic rubber similar to that of a two-piece ball and is just as hard. The middle layer is generally extremely thin and made of ionomers. The outer plastic cover can be thinner than most two-piece balls, and softer. As a result it sticks to the clubface a little better on shorter shots, which adds spin, although thinner covers are also more apt to tear.

In order to keep the aerodynamics optimal, the ball needs to be clean. Golfers can wash their balls manually, but there are also mechanical ball washers available.

THE 4-PIECE BALL: Best for Stronger Players Four-piece balls are generally recommended for players with faster swings. Typically, it has the same hard inner rubber core as two- and three-piece balls, but is surrounded by a second, thinner layer of rubber to soften the feel. It contains two outer layers, one made of ionomer and one of hard plastic. This allows the manufacturer to tweak the characteristics of the ball. While these balls are often dubbed 'tour' or 'pro', it doesn't mean they're better overall.

59

Fat or Skinny?
WHICH IS RIGHT FOR YOU

Find a grip that works for you

If you struggle with a wristy stroke, try a fatter putter grip. A fatter grip makes it difficult for your wrists to participate in the stroke—which is a good thing.

A **Putter** that Fits

Putter fitting is just as important as any other club—maybe more important. After all, we use our putters more than twice as much as any other club. Variables in putter fitting involve static fitting options like height and arm length but also involve many personal fitting selections like putter alignment preferences and your stroke type. If you tend to stand tall at address you may need a more upright, longer putter than if you tended to bend over. If you tend to extend your arms you may need a shorter putter. It's a very personal thing.

Loft is also an important variable for your putter. Most putters have between 3 and 5 degrees of loft. The loft will affect how the ball comes off the putter and how long it skids before it starts its true roll. If you tend to play on slow greens with long grass you may want more loft to get the ball up on top of the grass and rolling smoothly.

"The right putter for YOU can help you sink more putts."

ON COURSE » 3 HOLES

PAR 5» 517 YARDS, PAR 4» 405 YARDS, PAR 3» 125 YARDS

WHAT REALLY GOES ON OUT THERE?

I would complain to my Pro that bad shot culprits cropped up not so much during my lesson or on the range, but always out on the course where I needed help the most. It's like going to the doctor because you are not feeling well, the day of the appointment, you feel great—no symptoms. So let's play a few holes together where we explore valuable shot saving lessons, plus learn tools and techniques so you can execute the shots you need. Our goal is to get you playing better out on the course, where it counts, so you can reach your goals!

YARDS: 517 TO PIN, NO. 1 HANDICAP HOLE, PIN MIDDLE

Working with the Enemy

Too many players head straight for the middle of the tee box without taking a good look at their options. Using the tee box to your advantage helps you make a full commitment to your intended target out in the fairway. First, be aware of where the tee box is aiming you because sometimes it is aimed directly into trouble. You can see on this tee box that it is, in fact, aiming me right into the massive fairway bunkers and the water. Next, determine the best angle visually. This will do a couple of things: (1) it will provide more confidence, and (2) you will minimize possible swing compensations to avoid the trouble.

Alignment on the tee is not to be taken lightly. It is not always a straight shot down the middle of the fairway. Sometimes, you may need to draw the ball off the tee to get the best second shot angle. Or perhaps a fade is better; for example, on a dogleg right hole. If you prefer to hit the ball without any special attention to a left-to-right or vice versa, then choose the best spot on the tee box to achieve this goal.

The Scenario

I have a long Par 5 ahead of me, but I am up for the challenge. Kevin is illustrating that it is not advantageous to set-up on the right side of the tee box because visually, I am aiming directly into trouble. Further, he explains, if I miss my tee shot left, I am going to find the fairway bunkers, or worse, the water hazard. A high risk shot with zero reward.

My first option: set-up on the left side and draw the ball into the fairway, avoiding the massive fairway bunkers and the water. The other option: I can hit it straight, but I am looking for max roll on this intimidating dogleg left. *What would you do?*

Watch this lesson
topic online!

YES

Set-up on the side of trouble; the water and the massive fairway bunkers. A good rule of thumb: side with the enemy. When you can't beat them—join them.

MY DECISION

I have decided I will shape my tee shot—a smart play. If you cannot beat the trouble, then join the trouble, on the same side. Setting up on the tee box on the left side and aiming out towards the right center of the fairway is a wise decision. From this point of view, visually, I have a wide-open landing area with trouble well to my left. So in essence, I am setting up with my back towards the trouble so I don't have to look at it. I have set-up on the tee for a high reward, low risk shot.

Watch this lesson
topic online!

ALIGNMENT & SUCH

HIT MORE FAIRWAYS WITH A GOOD SET-UP

ON THE BOX

GET SQUARE

❶▶ Intermediate Target

❷▶ An Alignment Issue

❸▶ Ball Position

One of the more important elements in shot-making is alignment. The Pros take considerable care when it comes to the alignment process. They know if they are not properly aligned to their selected target, then they will need to do some fancy maneuvers on the downswing in order to redirect the ball back towards the target.

You may be wondering, "If they think they are aimed correctly, then why would they need to compensate?" The answer is simple. Your body is very smart. It knows, even if your brain doesn't: "Hey there, why are you aiming so far right when the target is this way, you dummy. Fine, now I have to work harder—no fun!"

If you would like to make the alignment process a piece of cake, then I suggest you learn how to do it right. We'll also discuss ball position in this section for good measure.

STEP 1

Select your target out in the fairway. Next, select your intermediate target that is inline with your fairway target, but just a few inches in front of you.

STEP 2

Step in with your right foot with your body behind the ball, aiming the clubface to your intermediate target.

Most good players use an intermediate target as an alignment aid. An intermediate target is a leaf or blade of grass a few feet or inches in front of the ball that is used to set the clubface.

STEP 3

Ensure that your intermediate target is inline with your fairway target. Here, my main target is the last palm tree on the right, and the white circle illustrates my intermediate target.

71

STEP 4

Set your feet, hips and shoulders parallel and left of the target line.

STEP 5

GRIP it LIGHT and RIP it!

Christina's 24

I dropped my right foot back just a bit in my set-up to promote a draw.

"Are you 'choking the chicken'?"

Guys, be careful: your tendency is to grip the club too tight, and swing too hard. Instead, grip it lightly, and swing at eighty percent of your normal swing speed for more accuracy, and fewer slices.

2► ALIGNMENT & SUCH

AN ALIGNMENT ISSUE

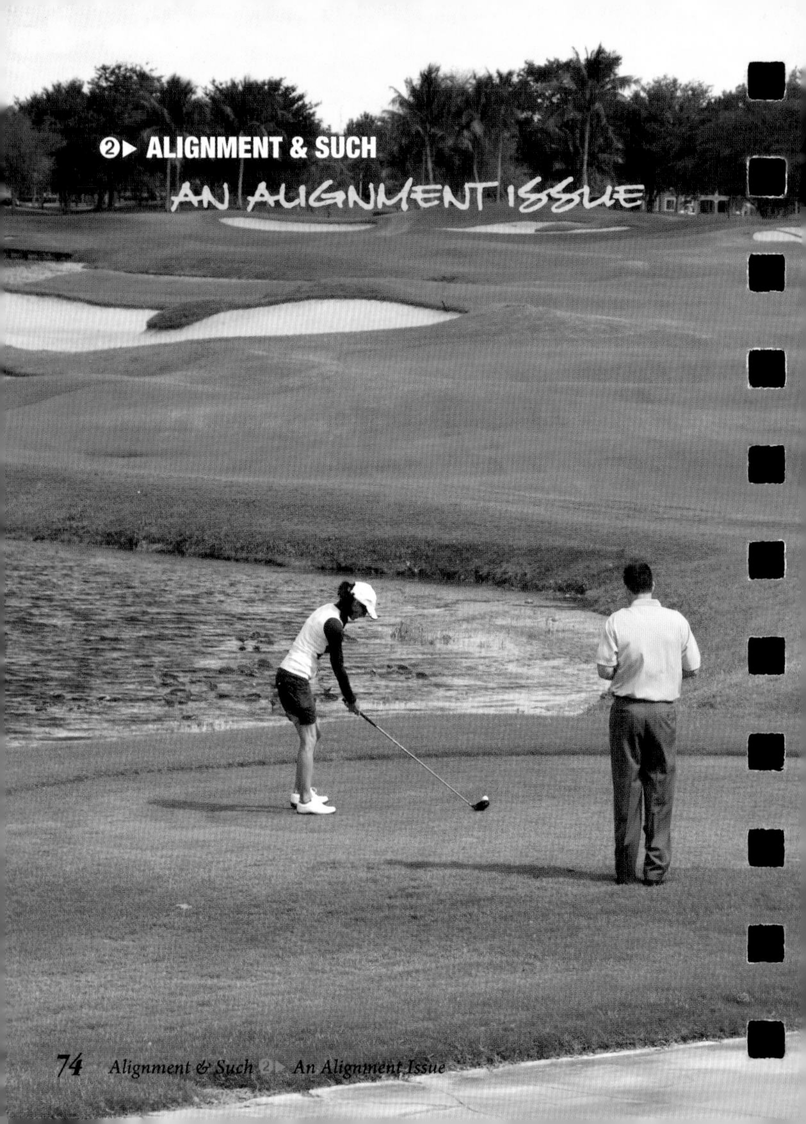

What's wrong with this picture?

HINT: IT'S ALL IN YOUR SET-UP!

THE PROBLEM

I am set-up on the correct side of the tee box. My clubface is set to my intended target so what's the problem? My feet, hips and shoulders are open. This means they are not SQUARE to the target line but aiming too far left. I will either hit a slice (left-to-right ball flight that goes nowhere), or I will try to redirect by blocking my shot to the right.

THE SOLUTION

Your goal is to set your bodylines, (feet, knees, hips forearms and shoulders) so they are parallel and left of the target line. Visualize a set of railroad tracks. Your feet, knees, hips and shoulders are on one side of the tracks, and the clubhead and ball are on the opposite side of the tracks.

POSSIBLE CULPRITS:

1. You did not follow the alignment procedure on the previous pages.
2. You took your practice swing at address. Instead, take your practice swing from behind the ball looking out towards the target. Then walk into the shot.
3. You set-up fine, and then opened your shoulders. *Learn more in* TEE BOX BASICS» *Page 164.*

77

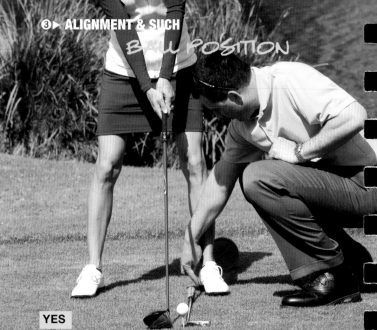

BALL POSITION

YES

DRIVER: Position off your left heel to promote an upward strike. If it is positioned too far back, you will not achieve much airtime or distance. An exception would be if you are playing into a strong wind. *Learn more in* TEE BOX BASICS» *Page 156.*

> *"... more fat shots are caused by players positioning the ball too far forward than by making a poor swing. If the ball is anywhere in your stance other than where you intend to have your swing bottom out, you will be forced to make compensations that will sacrifice your consistency."* - DAVE PELZ

Q. How important is Ball Position?

A. Very!

Watch this lesson topic online!

The Importance of Ball Position

Many players give only a casual acknowledgement to ball position. If it is somewhere in the vicinity of my two feet it should be fine. If neglected, it can cause a plethora of problems leading to poor contact and alignment issues. For example, if the ball is placed too far forward in your stance, it is very easy to slide rather than turn through impact, leading to an erratic ball flight or a shot that balloons into the air.

In addition, our eyes can get accustomed to a certain ball position, it just starts to look 'right' and therefore, we assume that our ball position is fine, but a majority of the time it is not. The best way to check your ball position is to set up to a golf ball as if you were about to hit it, then have a friend place a club between your feet, perpendicular to your target line, as shown. From this position, it is very easy to see the middle of your stance and your ball position in relation to this point.

YES

Set-up square if you are very flexible.

Kevin suggests a flared foot to promote a better torso rotation and speed through the ball. If you are flexible, square both feet to prevent any lateral movement in the backswing or downswing. However, if you are less flexible, flare both feet between 20-45 degrees for speed and power.

YES

Flare your left foot for
more speed and power.

Christina's **24**

🌱 Vary your ball
/ position around
the green to
achieve different
trajectories.

DRIVER: The ball should be aligned
off your left heel.

WOODS/HYBRIDS: The ball should
be aligned left of center, 1-2 inches
off your left heel.

2-6 Iron: The ball should be aligned left of center, 2-3
inches off your left heel.

SW-PW up to 7 Iron: The ball should be positioned in
the middle of your stance.

Putter: The ball should be positioned depending on
your putter's loft. *Learn more in* PUTTING BASICS≫
Page 260.

UNLEASH YOUR POWER
LEARN POWER ZAPPERS OFF THE TEE
WITH BARRY GOLDSTEIN

UNLEASH YOUR POWER

①▶ Stance & Hands

②▶ Backswing Power Leaks

③▶ Downswing Power Leaks

④▶ Finish for Power

❶▶ UNLEASH YOUR POWER

STANCE & HANDS

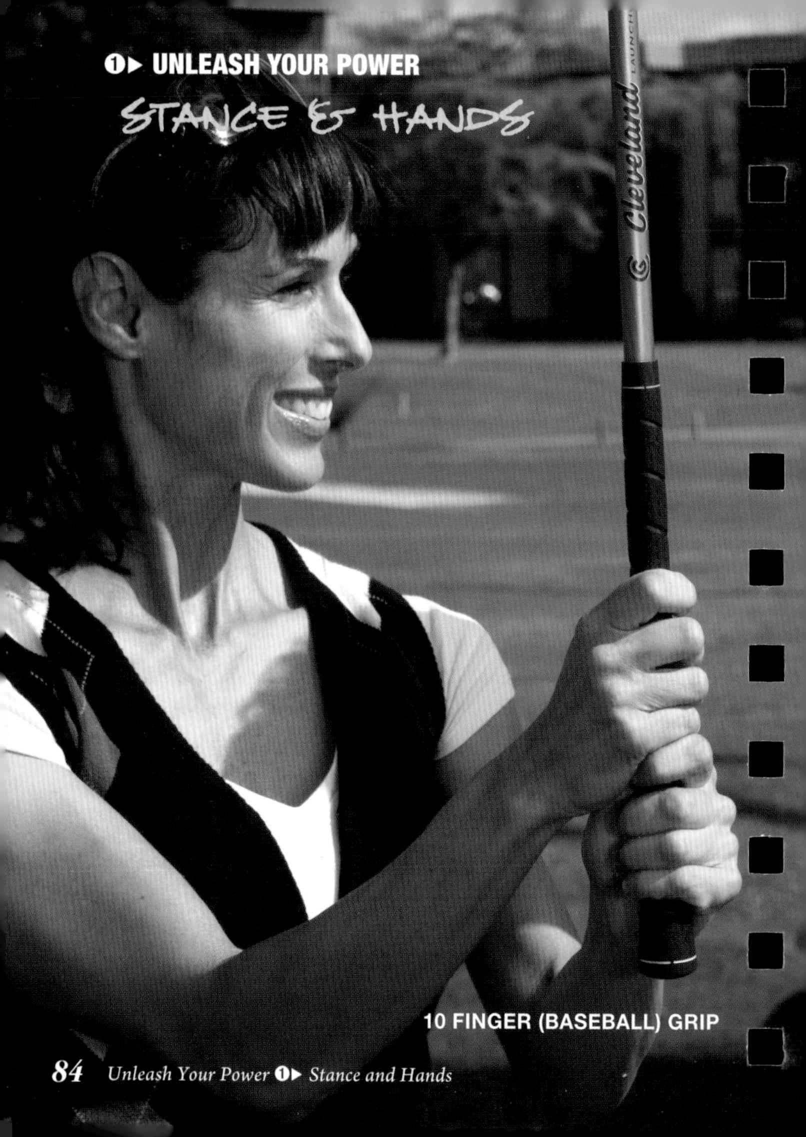

10 FINGER (BASEBALL) GRIP

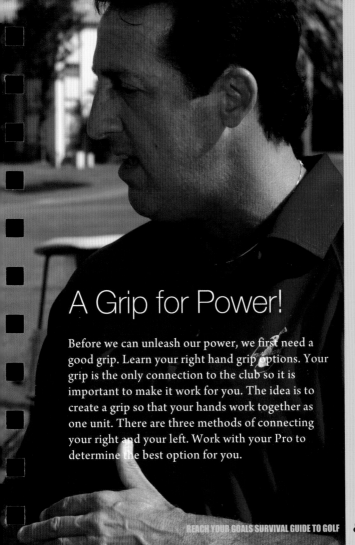

A Grip for Power!

Before we can unleash our power, we first need a good grip. Learn your right hand grip options. Your grip is the only connection to the club so it is important to make it work for you. The idea is to create a grip so that your hands work together as one unit. There are three methods of connecting your right and your left. Work with your Pro to determine the best option for you.

YES
A strong grip: both V's point to somewhere between my right ear and shoulder.

Make sure your V's line up

Your hands need to work together, not independently. Ideally, your V's created by your thumb and index finger match. If they do not, you will experience erratic shots: shots that go left, shots that go right, and in-between. I often monitor my grip because sometimes it gets sloppy. So keep an eye on yours!

1 THE 10 FINGER GRIP is popular with women and junior golfers. It provides the most support.

2 THE OVERLAP GRIP is popular with professional golfers. The pinkie of your right hand overlaps the index finger of your left hand.

3 THE INTERLOCK, the grip I use. The pinkie finger of your right hand interlocks with the index finger of left hand.

1
10 FINGER (BASEBALL) GRIP

2
OVERLAP

3
INTERLOCK

NO

A base that is too narrow does not provide enough stability to support a driver swing.

Power Stance

Barry believes in establishing an athletic base, which begins from the ground up. Set your feet wide for power. A good rule of thumb is slightly wider than shoulder-width.

Watch this lesson topic online!

YES

A wider base provides more stability and athleticism.

Christina's

I sit into my hips and check this with my right hand during set-up.

NO

Hands set too far forward will deloft the clubface making it virtually impossible to deliver an upward strike.

Driver and Hand Position

Our goal is an upward strike into the back of the ball with your driver. Your set-up must complement this objective with a wide base and the correct hand and ball position.

Watch this lesson topic online!

YES

An ideal hand position is inline with your hands or slightly back of center.

NO

Lifting your left foot
narrows the distance
between my knees
and provides minimal
coil. Coil is the
relationship between
your lower body and
upper body in the
backswing.

❷▶ UNLEASH YOUR POWER

BACKSWING LEAKS

Plant Your Feet for Power

Your feet play a vital role for a solid backswing. Ideally, you would like to feel the weight on the inside of your feet (instep) at the top of your backswing. If you are less flexible it may be a challenge to keep your left foot firmly planted.

YES

If you are flexible enough, it is best to keep your left foot firmly planted in your backswing. This helps create that power coil for good distance.

Christina's 2¢

Place a soccer ball between your knees to promote wide knees.

93

Don't Fake it...

45°

40°

NO

The 'Fake Turn Syndrome' is a common fault in the backswing. Instead, turn so your back is fully facing the target.

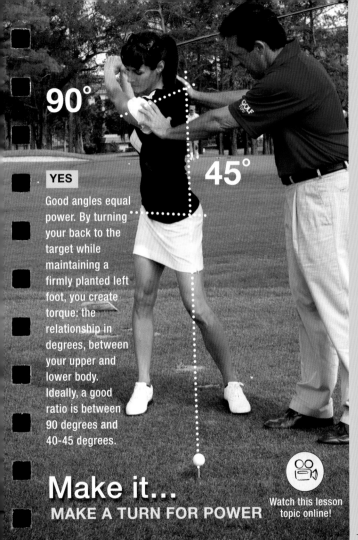

90°

45°

YES

Good angles equal power. By turning your back to the target while maintaining a firmly planted left foot, you create torque: the relationship in degrees, between your upper and lower body. Ideally, a good ratio is between 90 degrees and 40-45 degrees.

Make it...
MAKE A TURN FOR POWER

Watch this lesson topic online!

Notice how my hips have moved laterally to the right creating a V with my right leg. This is a result of letting my weight shift to the outside my right foot.

A Tight Circle

A good visualization is to feel like you are turning in a circle the width of your hips—a mini hoola-hoop. You goal is to turn within the circle and not move outside of it. If you move outside the circle, you will lose leverage and experience power failure, meaning you will have lost your coil between your upper and lower body.

YES

Ideally, turn into your right hip and make sure you feel pressure on the INSIDE of your right foot.

DOWNSWING LEAKS

NO

The clubhead will win the race if the clubhead reaches the ball before your hands. You will have unleashed your power and have nothing left to release through impact.

YES

Holding your angles in the downswing is what creates that incredible pop, where the ball flies off the clubface at warp speed. This can only happen if you maintain your lag.

Watch this lesson topic online!

Maintain Your Lag

Unless you are going fishing, the term 'casting'—defined as releasing your angles early, or more simply stated, throwing the club from the top—results in less power through impact.

Learn more in TEE BOX BASICS» *Page 170.*

My back is still facing towards the target.

Let your legs initiate while your back is still facing the target.

YES

The beauty of the downswing is if your backswing was a success then the downswing just happens. It's the rubber band effect or a spring loading and then unloading. You are just going for the ride. Your do not have to make a conscious effort except to get to your finish!

Be a Swinger, Not a Hitter

As you are finishing your turn in the backswing, your lower body initiates the downswing. This change of direction is what creates the lag. Most players feel like they have to help with this endeavor by getting overactive with their release. They hit at the ball instead of letting the momentum created by their leg drive produce the movement through the swing.

How's Your Finish?

NO

An off-balance finish will typically result in a high, weak right ball flight, or a slice.

NO

My weight has not transferred properly to my front side. Instead, I have fallen back and off balance.

❹▶ UNLEASH YOUR POWER

FINISH FOR POWER

A great finish not only looks good, it helps you make a better swing and play better golf. Even if the shot was a disgrace, get to a full finish and hold it for three seconds, or until the ball lands.

YES

With a good finish, the majority of your weight is on the outside of your left foot and your right knee is touching or almost touching your left leg.

Incorporating this finish routine into *your* routine will accomplish two very important things:

❶▶ A full finish keeps you and the clubhead moving through so you are making a swing with acceleration. ❷▶ It creates consistency in your swing. Finishing the same every time, even if the shot was less than desirable, ingrains good habits that will translate to good shots, or at least, good misses.

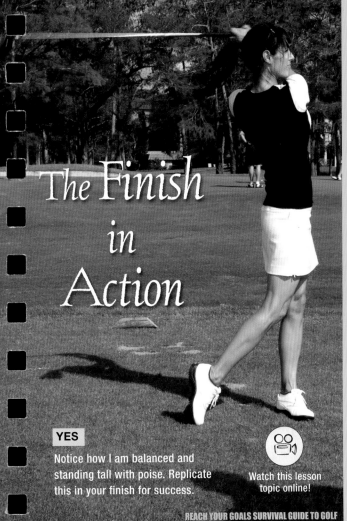

The Finish in Action

YES

Notice how I am balanced and standing tall with poise. Replicate this in your finish for success.

Watch this lesson topic online!

ON COURSE » PAR 5

THINK TWO SHOTS AHEAD

YES

A good method of determining club selection for your second shot is to ask yourself what club do you want to hit on your third shot?

The Scenario

I have hit a good drive on this challenging Par 5. A bogey is a good score on this hole; Par is awesome. I have bunkers running down the right side of the fairway with water occupying the entire left side. If I hit my 3-wood perfectly, I can get to 87 yards for an easy wedge. However, if I miss even a little, I am in the water, or one of the bunkers—not a high percentage shot. A better option: hit my hybrid to 112 and then use a PW into the green.

OPTION 1:

Hit my 3-wood here and hope I hit it perfectly.

OPTION 2:

Lay-up here and avoid all the trouble.

THE SOLUTION

Kevin and I determined that I should take the high percentage shot, Option 2, and eliminate the trouble.

My drive landed here.

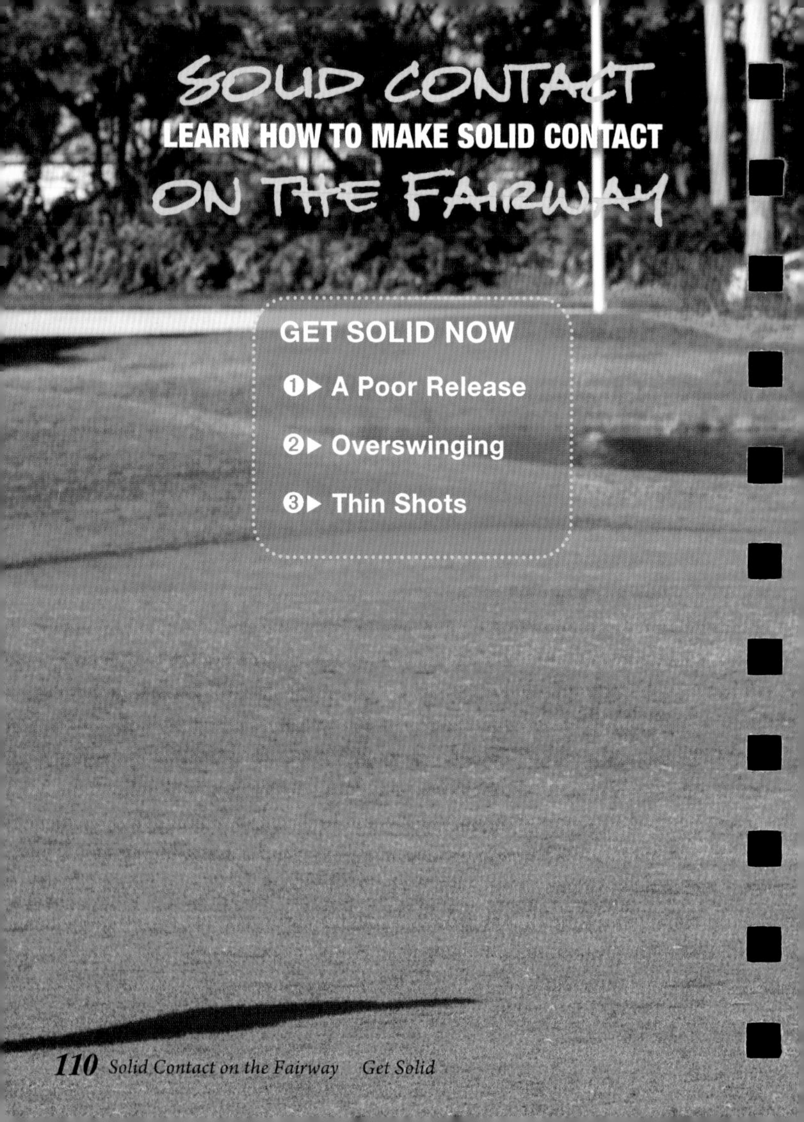

SOLID CONTACT

LEARN HOW TO MAKE SOLID CONTACT

ON THE FAIRWAY

GET SOLID NOW

❶▶ A Poor Release

❷▶ Overswinging

❸▶ Thin Shots

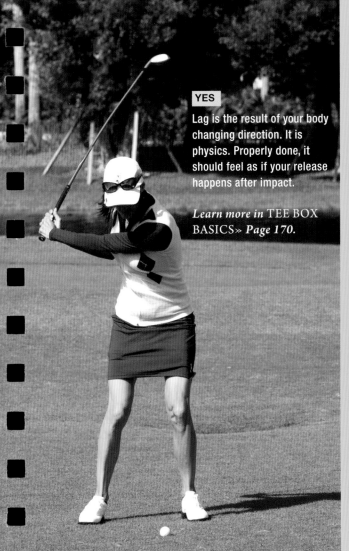

YES

Lag is the result of your body changing direction. It is physics. Properly done, it should feel as if your release happens after impact.

Learn more in TEE BOX BASICS» *Page 170.*

A POOR RELEASE

The 'Chicken Wing' Release
What causes this dreaded release?

Tension is a big culprit. Others may include: not folding your left arm correctly through the release; getting stuck as a result of fast hips; alignment; trying to redirect and guide the club to the intended target; or a weak grip. Another culprit may be your downswing move. If you do not transfer your weight to your left side, but fall away from the target, you will experience the 'chicken'. If your body slows down or decelerates through impact, you will most likely experience the 'chicken'.

SOLUTIONS

Try this: *Throw the Club* drill is a great test to determine your tension levels. Find this drill on page 314. Another solution that worked for me and I still use to maintain a connected back and follow-through is the *Towel Drill*. Find this drill on page 340.

NO

YES

A good release will allow your right forearm to crossover your left through impact to your finish.

Watch this lesson topic online!

❷▶ SOLID CONTACT
OVERSWINGING

The backswing sets the stage for a powerful downswing. One cannot happen without the other for consistent results. One of the main culprits is overswinging. It does a couple of not-so-pretty things:

❶ Overswinging results in a club that goes past parallel, which produces a disconnected backswing.

❷ My left arm has collapsed shortening my arc radius, a result of my shoulders not completing the turn.

❸ Overswinging takes me out of my posture. I have lost my coil which is needed for power and speed in the downswing.

❹ Overswinging kept too much weight on my left side, which can produce a reverse pivot.

Watch this lesson topic online!

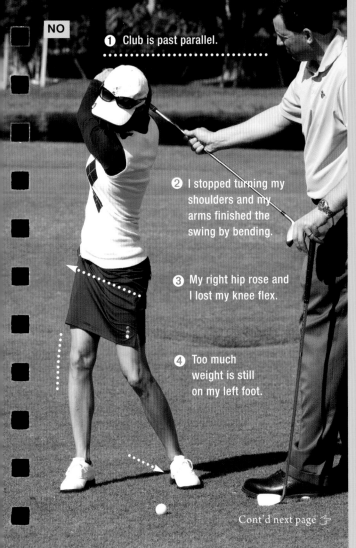

NO

1. Club is past parallel.

2. I stopped turning my shoulders and my arms finished the swing by bending.

3. My right hip rose and I lost my knee flex.

4. Too much weight is still on my left foot.

Cont'd next page

YES

① My club is barely at parallel.

② My left arm is straight, not rigid.

③ I am sitting into my right hip and feeling the pressure on the inside of my right thigh.

④ My weight has transferred to the inside of my right foot.

You should feel loaded in your backswing like a stretched rubber. I like to feel my center of gravity low and maintain this feeling through the backswing and into the start of the downswing. This virtually eliminates thin shots for me.

❶ I have made a nice coil with my shoulders and my arms are working together as one unit—a connected backswing.

❷ My left arm is extended and straight, not rigid, creating a wide arc.

❸ I turned into my right hip and feel the pressure on the inside of my right thigh. My right knee remains flexed at the top of my backswing.

❹ My weight has transferred to the inside of my right heel. I feel pressure on my instep, like I am bearing down into the turf.

Christina's Advice: "I see more women struggle with overswinging than men; most likely due to strength. A method that worked for me when I had this issue was to feel like you are making a three-quarter backswing, or even better, a half backswing. It will feel short, but it will be a complete backswing. Have a buddy watch you the next time you tee off so she can confirm this for you. Keep in mind: your tempo may quicken simply because your timing will be off, but keep with it."

③ ▶ SOLID CONTACT
THIN SHOTS

In the early days, I wish I had a better understanding of how the ball actually gets airborne. It's called compression, trapping the ball between the clubface and the turf, which will result in a divot on the forward side of the ball. I became a great 'picker', one who picked the ball cleanly off the turf. When I connected, it felt pure, but most of the time I would hit the ball thin. I still have to consciously remind myself to hit down and through and take a divot. We want a divot—it's a good thing—as long as it's shallow like a dollar bill and on the forward side of the ball.

Imagine the ball is in the way of your swing. If you hit down and not through, you will most likely chunk the ball as a result of decelerating and your divot will be on the backside of the ball.

Christina's 2¢

Love your divots, but keep in mind you need to hit down AND through the ball.

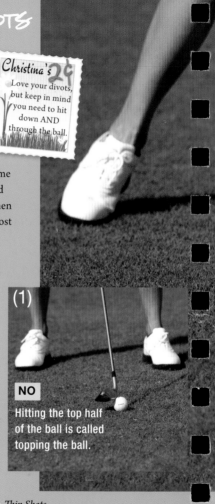

(1)

NO

Hitting the top half of the ball is called topping the ball.

What THIN looks like

NO

I have picked the ball cleanly, no divot.

(2)

THE ANATOMY OF A THIN SHOT

Thin is defined as the opposite of compression. You either hit the top half of the ball (1), or graze the grass creating no divot (2), usually a low shot that veers right. On the next page (3), I compressed the ball and my reward—it pops off the club.

YES

Notice how my hands are still slightly ahead, which allows for a descending blow.

(3)

What SOLID *Looks Like*

THE ANATOMY OF A SOLID SHOT

I compressed the ball and my reward—it pops off the club. I create a divot as a result of hitting down and through the turf, keeping my hands slightly ahead through the hitting area.

Watch this lesson
topic online!

OPTION 1:

Hit my PW to a tight pin and putt for birdie.

Pro Tip: *"Confidence is the key ingredient with any shot, whether you are laying-up or going for a tight pin. If you commit one hundred percent, meaning zero doubt, then chances of success are higher."*

- Kevin Sprecher

PATH OF LEAST RESISTANCE

OPTION 2:

Go for the fat part of the green for a 2-putt.

The Scenario

My second shot with a hybrid was a success. I am now 112 from the pin. Now, I have some decisions to make. Do I go for the pin and have a chance at a birdie putt, or do I go for the fat part of the green?

What would you do?

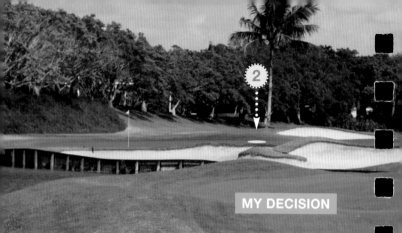

MY DECISION

I have decided to go with a higher percentage shot; go for the fat part of the green, Option 2. I made this choice because the risk of Option 1 was not worth the reward. The pin is tucked on the far left corner of the green surrounded by water and large greenside bunkers. There is also a right-to-left wind. If I miss-hit even a little, I am in trouble and a double or triple for sure—no thanks.

For a high trajectory, for example to a tight pin, I will finish with my hands higher.

YES

124

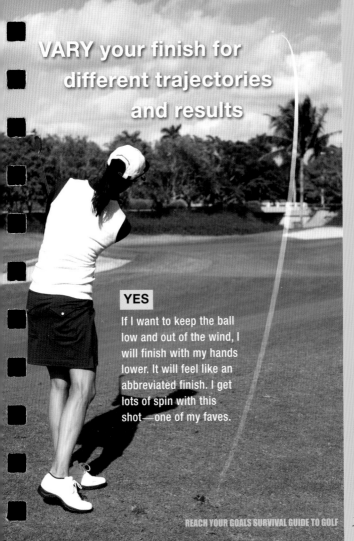

VARY your finish for different trajectories and results

YES

If I want to keep the ball low and out of the wind, I will finish with my hands lower. It will feel like an abbreviated finish. I get lots of spin with this shot—one of my faves.

ON THE GREEN

Pro Tip: *"A common error with downhill putts: players do not choose the right spot where the ball will begin to drop towards the hole. With breaking putts, it is better to select a spot slightly higher on the intended line than too low. Your putt will never have a chance on the 'low side'."*

— *Kevin Sprecher*

I chose Option 2 and my approach shot was perfect. I landed in a low risk area of the green. I am left with a downhill putt for Par, challenging, but makeable.

In fact, I do make 2 putts for my Par. Let's examine on the following pages how to read breaking, downhill putts so you can make your Par too.

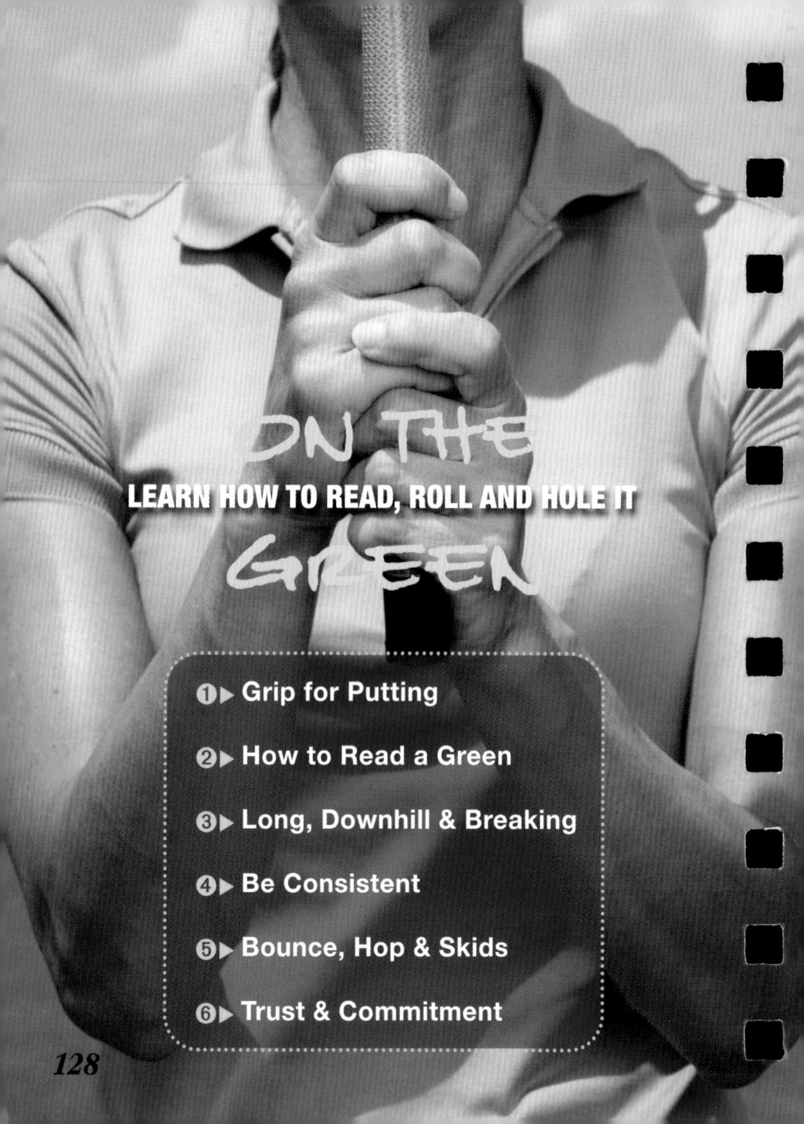

ON THE

LEARN HOW TO READ, ROLL AND HOLE IT

GREEN

1 ▶ Grip for Putting

2 ▶ How to Read a Green

3 ▶ Long, Downhill & Breaking

4 ▶ Be Consistent

5 ▶ Bounce, Hop & Skids

6 ▶ Trust & Commitment

128

Claw, Box, Left-Hand Low?

You may be thinking, "Why the heck do I need a different grip for putting?" The answer is simple. The main culprit of missed putts are overactive wrists. We need control, not power in our putting stroke, which will provide the consistency we need to have fewer than 32 putts a round.

The key to solid putting is quiet hands. The hands, wrists, and arms act as one unit. By taking the proper putting grip, you, in essence, take your wrists out of the stroke. This gives you the best chance of hitting the sweet spot, the center of the putterface, and of course, making the putt.

Now putting is interesting because it allows for more unique styles of grips. There is not just one way to grip the putter, but the most common is the Reverse Overlap, which is the grip I use.

I use the Reverse Overlap grip. (shown here)

A Popular Choice

Reverse Overlap

The Reverse Overlap grip is a popular choice among players. The index finger of my left hand overlaps the last three fingers of my right and my palms are parallel to each other. This gives me a quiet, wristless stroke.

» Left-hand-low grip (also known as Cross-handed, Crossover (shown here)

Other grips include:

» Claw grip

» The Box grip

» Split-handed grip

» Palms facing grip

» The Pencil grip for a long putter

» Two Fingers Down grip (shown here)

Watch this lesson topic online!

HOW TO READ THE GREEN

Reading the Green

You begin reading the green as you are walking up or driving towards the green. A wide angle gives you the best angle and lay of the land, specifically, the overall slope of the green. On this green you can see the slope falls towards the water. You will also notice it is a two-tiered green. My ball landed on the upper tier. I have a downhill, left-to-right putt.

Christina's 2¢

If you focus only on putting your handicap will drop.

Lower tier

Upper tier breaking left-to-right with a downhill slope

Check the Cup
Look for the shaggy side

This is the way the grain is growing. When putting with the grain, expect the ball to roll more quickly. Against the grain, slower. Depending on the type of grass, you can also look for the shiny side of the grain. If you're putting with the shine, it will roll faster. If you are putting against the shine, slower.

Kevin is showing me how to determine the grain. Keep in mind, this is not allowed during a round.

Shaggy Side

Against the grain

Brown shag is on this side of the cup, so the grain is going from Kevin towards the water.

Down grain towards water

Shaggy Side

135

A Side and Wide Angle

Another good idea: cut the hole in half, but from a side view. You can clearly see the slope and how much the green breaks from this perspective.

Christina's Advice: "I always like to view the slope from down the target line, the side view shown here, as well as from behind the hole looking back towards my ball. However, I only check all angles if I have time. For pace of play, I check behind the hole and target line."

Kevin is showing me how easy it is to see the slope.

For the super-long, breaking, downhill scary putts; cut the hole in sections, so the hole becomes less intimidating. Look for big breaks towards the initial part of the putt. Also, look at the last five feet of the hole. This is where the ball will break most as it begins to slow down.

Watch this lesson topic online!

BE CONSISTENT

STEP 1

Determine the slope and break by standing five feet or more behind your ball. If you stand too close, it is difficult to see the break.

YES

You can see the slope better if you get low as Kevin and I have here.

140

STEP 2

Find the fall line where the putt will begin to drop towards the hole.

HOW TO BE A CONSISTENT PUTTER
5 steps to get it close for breaking putts

The first step to being a consistent putter is to establish a pre-putt routine. A routine sets the stage for a consistent plan of action every time you prepare to stroke a putt.

141

STEP 4

I focus on the hole for feel and on my intermediate spot for line. I trust and stroke the putt with even tempo back and through.

STEP 3

I pick a spot a few inches in front of me. I use this to get the ball rolling on my intended line.

STEP 5

No peeking! Be sure to watch the putt, but only after you have stroked it. Watch how the ball reacts if it passes the hole, because you are coming back on that same line.

BOUNCE HOP & SKIDS

THIS BALL IS ROLLING
A good roll has no spin, which is exactly what we need for consistent putting.

Do you suffer from the bounce, hop or skids?

Have you ever noticed how the ball comes off the putterface when you putt? Do your putts roll smoothly, or do they seem to bounce to the hole? Does the ball skid or squirt off the putterface like its had too much to drink? Putts do not like spin. Spin is what causes the bounce, hop and skid effect. To avoid these deadly rolls that throw your putt offline, be sure that the ball is positioned correctly based on the loft of your putter. *Learn more in* PUTTING BASICS» *Page 260*. Also, a jerky tempo will cause the ball to go offline.

Watch this lesson topic online!

THIS BALL IS AIRBORNE
Most likely the result of ball position at address, the path of the stroke, peeking, or tempo.

TRUST & COMMITMENT

NO

DO NOT BE FEARFUL

Never let a putt intimidate you.
Establish a pre-putt routine, one
you can trust and commit to, and
putts will drop.

Your New Mantra

"I love my putting, I am a great putter."

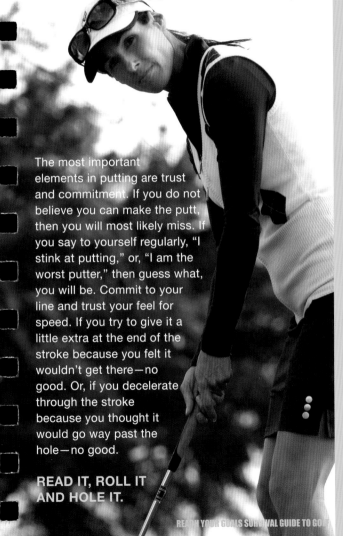

The most important elements in putting are trust and commitment. If you do not believe you can make the putt, then you will most likely miss. If you say to yourself regularly, "I stink at putting," or, "I am the worst putter," then guess what, you will be. Commit to your line and trust your feel for speed. If you try to give it a little extra at the end of the stroke because you felt it wouldn't get there—no good. Or, if you decelerate through the stroke because you thought it would go way past the hole—no good.

READ IT, ROLL IT AND HOLE IT.

ON COURSE » PAR 4

YARDS: 405 TO PIN, NO. 13 HANDICAP HOLE, PIN FRONT

EVERY SHOT DEMANDS
YOUR ATTENTION

Golf is a demanding game because it requires every
bit of you. The good news is, you have a choice.
The challenge is to select the right shot at the right
time. Let's play a Par 4 together and learn how to
make smart decisions from tee to green.

How far is the trouble?

OPTION 1:

The bunkers are 265 yards out. I can aim here and take the water out of play.

(1)

OPTION 2:

I need to hit my driver perfectly to carry the 230 yards over water.

2

The Scenario

Know where your trouble is. We know the water is trouble, that's the easy part. But what about the fairway bunkers out in the fairway? Will they come into play? Can I reach them? How far is it to carry the water? If I clear the water, I can cut the hole in half for a short iron approach into the green. The point is, know how far you carry the ball with your driver so you can make an educated decision.

What shot would you choose?

151

MY DECISION

I have decided to take the water out of play and go with Option 1. My second shot will be longer but I would rather avoid a water penalty. I tee the ball on the side of trouble, the right side of the tee box.

Be honest with your yardages. I see, too often, players attempting shots, especially off the tee, they have no business trying. Examine risk versus reward, not, "I can make it, if I swing really hard."

TEE BOX

SET-UP FOR SUCCESS

BASICS

①▶ How to Play Wind

②▶ Practice Swings

③▶ Should You Hover?

④▶ Set-up for Distance

⑤▶ Downswing Basics

NO

NORMAL DRIVER SET-UP

My ball is positioned off my left heel and my arms are inline with the shaft.

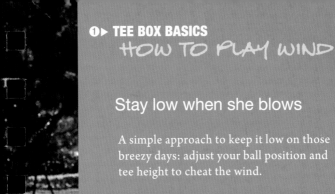

HOW TO PLAY WIND

Stay low when she blows

A simple approach to keep it low on those breezy days: adjust your ball position and tee height to cheat the wind.

NO

NORMAL TEE HEIGHT
This set-up will promote
an upward strike.

157

Keep it below the wind in the fairway

The key to controlling distance against a strong wind in the fairway is to take more club and swing easy which reduces spin. Backspin is what we do not want on a gusty day.

YES

A LOWER TEE HEIGHT promotes a level strike and a lower ball flight.

Christina's 2¢

Swing easy when it's breezy! If you fight the wind you will lose.

YES

WINDY DAY
I like a slightly wider stance when it's really blowing. My hands are set slightly ahead and the ball slightly back in my stance to promote a slight descending blow that helps keep the ball low.

159

PRACTICE SWINGS

Take your practice swing from behind the ball

In my early days, I would take my practice swing at address and then just readdress the ball and go—I thought this was the smart play. I later learned that taking your practice swing at address might lead to a misaligned set-up; meaning your feet, hips or shoulders can get out of position.

YES

I like to take my practice swing from behind the ball and then walk into to the ball from behind looking out towards the target.

NO

Taking a practice swing at address may lead to poor alignment.

NO

Grounding the club at address creates a change in grip pressure.

❸▶ TEE BOX BASICS

Should you hover?

Many Pros suggest that you hover the driver at address. I agree. Here are two good reasons. First, the driver never touches the ground through impact, so why would you address it this way? Second, to initiate your take-away you would need to lift the club, which may produce a tighter grip pressure—a distance killer.

Christina's

Keep your hover routine consistent for better contact.

YES

Hovering the club at address allows you to feel the clubhead and maintain a consistent grip pressure for a smooth take-away.

SET-UP FOR DISTANCE

SQUARE AT ADDRESS

NO

AN OPEN ADDRESS

A problem I continually
struggle with; I set-up square,
but then my shoulders open,
pointing left of my target line. I
lose distance with this set-up.

YES

A SQUARE ADDRESS

To correct this, I like to visualize my feet, knees, hips and shoulders on one side of the railway tracks and the clubhead and ball on the opposite side of the track, page 77.

STEP 1

Lower body initiates the downswing.

STEP 2

My feet and legs are driving into the ground.

Anatomy of an

YES: LEG DRIVE FOR POWER!

Inside Path

STEP 3

A powerful release
of the clubhead.
Notice, how the
ball starts right.

STEP 1

Upper body initiates the downswing.

STEP 2

My feet and legs are quiet. I am not creating any leverage.

Anatomy of an

NO: LOWER BODY POWER LEAK

Outside Path

STEP 3

This ball will have a left-to-right ball flight, will have a high spin rate and the ball will start left of its target line.

YES

DRIVE DOWN FOR POWER

On the downswing, feel your center of gravity drive down into the turf with your legs, creating a squat like appearance. This leg drive drops the club down on an inside path ready for a powerful delivery through impact.

NO

Releasing the power. Do not throw the club outside on the downswing plane.

Drive Down, Not Out

You see all great players with great leg action on the downswing. It almost looks like they are squatting just before impact when they explode all their energies through the impact zone.

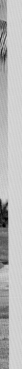

171

Post for Power

We hear lots about posting up on your left leg through impact, but what does that actually mean? It translates to creating leverage for your upper body to release stored energy created by your backswing. Why does this create power?

Your legs act as a catapult for your upper body. Your downswing is initiated with your hips, core and legs shifting towards the target, which creates a rubberband effect. Your left leg drives into the ground and begins to straighten as the club reaches impact.

NO
I did not use my legs to drive into the ground. The result; a bent left leg through impact.

This firm left side creates a launching pad for your upper body to release and extend away from the body. This leg action is what generates clubhead speed, power, and, ultimately, distance.

YES

My left side is firm so my upper body can release without holding back. Do not simply straighten your left leg, but DRIVE your energy into the ground so you can create leverage.

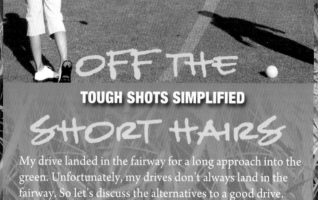

OFF THE

TOUGH SHOTS SIMPLIFIED

SHORT HAIRS

My drive landed in the fairway for a long approach into the green. Unfortunately, my drives don't always land in the fairway. So let's discuss the alternatives to a good drive.

❶▶ Hard Pan Lie
❷▶ Deep Rough
❸▶ Those Dang Trees
❹▶ Tall Grass

STEP 1

Take a wide base for more stability. Play the ball slightly back of center to ensure catching the ball first.

176

❶▶ OFF THE SHORT HAIRS

HARD PAN LIE

It's so tough, that's why they call it a 'Hard' Pan lie

You will find a lie like this in those vast fairway bunkers. What makes this shot tough? The lie, and of course, the tall grass that I need to dodge in this shot as well. Let's simplify this shot with the right set-up.

If just a punch out, then take a half backswing at half speed to ensure you stay in the shot.

STEP 3

The key to this shot is keeping your hands ahead through impact. Your finish will be low and abbreviated.

YES

Play the ball left of center. Your lie is good so you can make your normal swing. Make sure your transition and tempo are smooth.

Watch this lesson topic online!

HYBRID SET-UP

If your lie looks like this then use your hybrid. A great option out of the rough.

❷▸ OFF THE SHORT HAIRS

DEEP ROUGH

It's a rough lie, that's why they call it the 'Rough'.

The ball will have a tendency to go further with this lie so be sure to select the right landing area out in the fairway. Don't blindly hit out somewhere in the fairway. Be specific with your target landing area; for example, you get out, but end up on the opposite side, in deeper rough! Where is the benefit?

181

STEP 1

Play the ball slightly further back than you normally would to ensure catching the ball first.

IRON SET-UP

If half the ball or more is not visible, then your best bet is to use an iron and set-up for a steeper angle of attack. The key is to addres the ball with a slightly open set-up. At address, open your stance and clubface. This promotes an out-to-in path which cuts through the rough more easily.

YES

If your lie looks like this, then punch the ball out with an iron.

YES

An aggressive swing, down
and through, is required to get
the ball out of this deep rough.

STEP 3

STEP 2

Set-up with an open stance, and a slightly open clubface to ensure the face doesn't close through impact.

STEP 3

As you take the club back be sure to hinge your wrists. An aggressive swing to a complete finish will ensure you do not chop at the ball, but generate enough clubhead speed to get the ball out.

185

STEP 1

Set yourself as best you can. You want your lower body to remain quiet in this shot. Our goal is to punch the ball back into play.

❸▶ OFF THE SHORT HAIRS

THOSE DANG TREES

If you haven't found your way around a tree yet, you will. Let's get you out of trouble and on with your life.

Assess your lie carefully. Make sure you will not damage your club or yourself by attempting this shot. In addition, it is always a good idea to put your shades on to protect your eyes from flying tree debris. Mine are not on because I decided to take an unplayable—you may too.

Watch this lesson topic online!

187

Christina's 2¢

A half backswing
at half speed is
all you need.
Hey, that's a
good rhyme!

STEP 2

This shot is a 'punch out'
shot; a half backswing at half
speed is all you need. Make
sure your tempo is smooth—
don't jab at the ball.

"You are the only one who can say it is unplayable."

Should I take an 'Unplayable'?

That all depends on your lie and the surrounding area. If there is a root or rock, take an unplayable. The risk is not worth a stroke. Learn how to do it on the next page.

189

Take an Unplayable

Option 1

You can play a ball from the spot your original ball was last played, called 'stroke and distance.'

Option 2

You can drop a ball within two club lengths of where the ball lies, no closer to the hole.

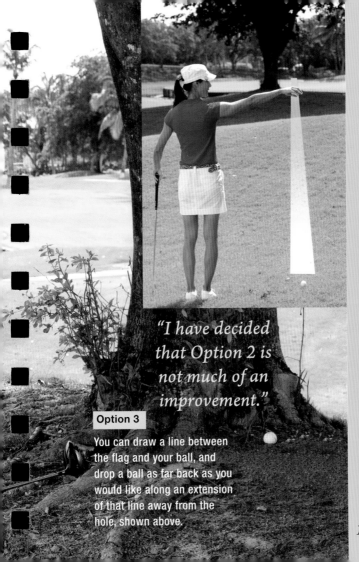

"I have decided that Option 2 is not much of an improvement."

Option 3

You can draw a line between the flag and your ball, and drop a ball as far back as you would like along an extension of that line away from the hole, shown above.

Putt it
Out

STEP 3

Release the putter on the follow-through and
the ball should come off the ground low, but
enough to get you out of trouble.

STEP 1

Set-up like you would for a putt. This shot requires hinge, so take your normal grip. Play the ball left of center; back in your stance.

STEP 2

Make a connected backswing like you are making a mammoth putt and hinge your wrists.

TALL GRASS

Get out in one shot. Don't compound the issue by trying to be a hero and attempt the green from here. Tall grass will have a tendency to close the face so take a firmer grip pressure. Another tendency is to try to help the ball in the air or come out of the shot early. Instead, focus on staying in the shot, hitting down steeply on the back of the ball.

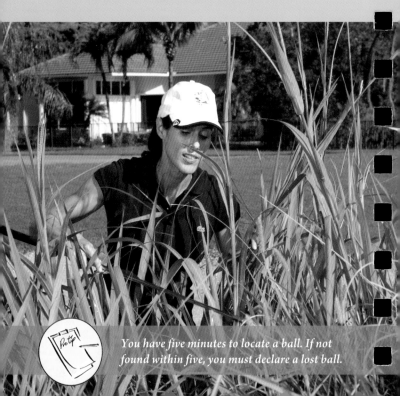

You have five minutes to locate a ball. If not found within five, you must declare a lost ball.

YES

GET STEEP AND FOCUSED
Use a lofted club like your 9-iron or
PW. With a slightly tighter grip
pressure, make a steep backswing
with lots of wrist hinge. Your follow-
through will be short if any,
depending on the condition of your lie. The ball
should pop out and back into the fairway.

Christina's **2¢**
Going
backwards
may be the
best option.

NO

If you select a club and you have even one percent doubt with that selection, your shot will most likely be a disappointment.

ON THE FAIRWAY

What shot would provide 100% confidence?

I have a long approach, 195 yards, into the green protected by water on the left side and greenside bunkers protecting the front of the green. My approach has to be accurate. There can be no doubt in my club selection. This shot will require absolute commitment and confidence.

My Options

OPTION 1:

Hit my 3-wood and go long, past the trouble, leaving myself a long putt.

OPTION 2:

Use a 5-iron and lay-up within 30 yards, then trust my wedge game to get up and down for Par.

What would you do?

197

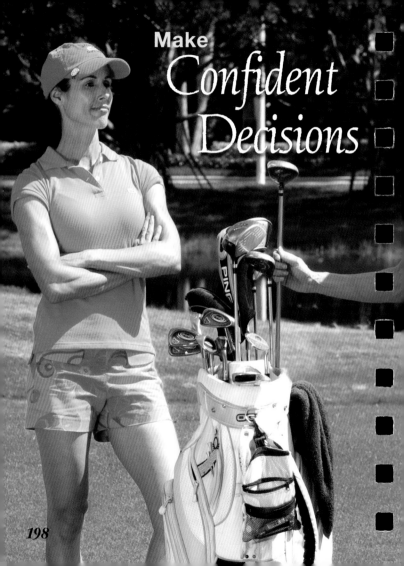

Make
Confident
Decisions

MY DECISION

I have decided to go with my 3-wood and fly the trouble. I am confident I can put a smooth swing using my 3-wood. If I am long that is fine. All the trouble is in front of the green, so long is good.

We will examine both options in case you decide to go for the lay-up—page 212.

YES

Select an exact landing spot on the green or around the green depending on your club choice. Make your intentions very clear, very positive, and no "dont's". There should be zero doubt—only one hundred percent confidence.

199

WOODS
SOLID IN THE FAIRWAY
& SET-UP

- ❶▶ Basic Set-up
- ❷▶ Head & Shoulders
- ❸▶ Get Square
- ❹▶ Take a Divot

YES

Your shaft should be inline with your hands and sternum. This set-up will maintain the club's loft and launch the ball high. It will be easier to square the club.

NO

Do not forward press. You are taking away the loft of the club (deloft). The ball flight will be low, right and most likely steep.

HEAD & SHOULDERS

NO

Level shoulders promotes a steeper descent on the downswing.

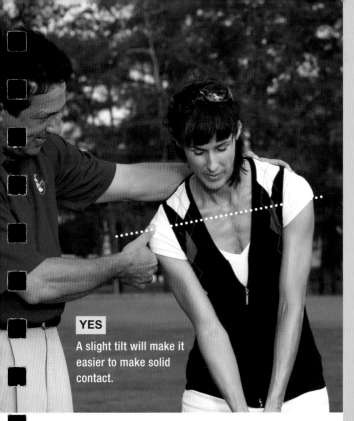

YES

A slight tilt will make it easier to make solid contact.

Tilt Your Shoulders

A slight tilt with your shoulders will promote solid contact with your fairway woods. Level shoulders have a tendency to promote a steeper angle on the downswing. A slight tilt will promote a more shallow path, producing a shallower divot.

203

NO

Head Position

A slight head tilt away from the target with your chin presets your eyes behind the ball, much like Jack Nicklaus did his entire career.

YES

Barry likes my chin pointing away from the target just slightly.

Christina's 2¢

Practice your wood set-up at home in front of a mirror.

With your eyes behind the ball, you will have less of a tendency to get steep on your downswing. And that's a good thing.

GET SQUARE

TARGET LINE

YES

A square face for
consistent shots.

Square-it-up with your face

What does a square face look like? This may seem like a simple answer but I see many players set-up to the ball with either a closed, 'shut' face, or an open face. Anything but square may result in compensations in the downswing to square up the face through impact.

TARGET LINE

NO
A closed face

TARGET LINE

NO
An open face

Barry is a big fan of divots, even with fairway woods. I was one who swept the ball off the grass with little or no divot. I would need to strike the ball perfectly, otherwise, my shot was typically thin. Barry suggested that my practice swing produce a divot with my woods, as well as, with my irons.

YES

Divots should be just after the ball, not before.

Watch this lesson topic online!

Why and Where Do Divots Happen?

Divots should appear after the ball, not before. A divot is a result of the clubhead coming into the ball on a slight descending blow, even with your woods. This compresses the ball. The bottom of the swing's arc is the divot.

NO

This divot is too deep and too big.

Women in particular, struggle with taking divots. Begin by taking divots with your practice swings. Keep in mind: divots are not intended to be deep, but shallow, like a dollar bill and always on the forward side of the ball.

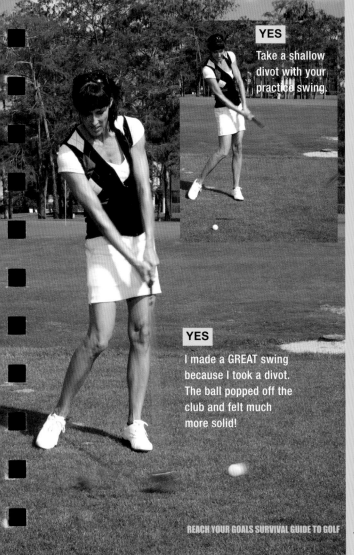

YES

Take a shallow divot with your practice swing.

YES

I made a GREAT swing because I took a divot. The ball popped off the club and felt much more solid!

Perhaps you would have selected a 5-iron instead of a 3-wood, a more conservative approach. Let's examine this approach. While we do that, let's also examine how to improve our irons and learn set-up for uneven lies.

GET IT RIGHT

Connection

+

Divot

=

Solid

OPTION 2:

Now let's select a 5-iron and lay-up within 30 yards. I will trust my wedge game to get up and down for Par.

STEP 1

It all begins with your grip pressure, keep it loose from the start of your swing to the finish.

5 IRON

STEP 2

I am staying in my posture and maintaining the solid connection created at address.

STEP 3

I am driving my feet and legs into the ground creating lots of clubhead speed. My connection is still intact.

STEP 4

Proof that I have hit down and through as indicated by the divot. My connection is still intact.

The moral of this tale: solid contact comes with loose muscles, an upper body connection and the driving force of your lower body that produces a divot on the forward side of the ball. Get these right for more greens in regulation and lower scores.

Follow the Slope
Uneven Lies

As we all know thanks to Columbus, the world is not flat, and neither are golf courses. Here's what you do if you find yourself with a ball above or below your feet.

A DOWNHILL SIDEHILL LIE

STEP 1

Pick the right target. In this case it's left not right. The ball will have a tendency to follow the slope so it will most likely fade off this lie, curve left-to-right. So choose a target left of where you would normally aim to accommodate for this tendency.

Watch this lesson
topic online!

STEP 2

Select one less club, as the ball will tend to go a bit further with this lie. Set-up to the ball by matching your spine angle with the slope. Because the ball is below your feet, you will need to bend more from the hips to reach the ball, or just stand closer to the ball. Play the ball in the center of your stance.

218

NO

The tendency is to want to scoop or help the ball in the air by leaning back at set-up.

STEP 3

Take a practice swing.

STEP 4

SWING WITH THE SLOPE
Swing down the slope well
past impact for solid contact.

YES

NO

Topping the ball is common with this shot.

The key to the success of this shot is staying in balance and in your posture, so swing at eighty percent of your normal swing speed. Topping the ball is common with this shot, simply because players fall off balance to help the ball in the air by swinging too hard. You should feel like you bent well over with this shot. This is the correct feeling. Simply maintain this feeling through the swing for solid contact.

221

BALL FLIGHT WILL FOLLOW SLOPE
The ball will have a tendency to follow the slope so it will most likely draw off this lie, curve right-to-left.

FOR A BALL ABOVE YOUR FEET

STEP 1

Select the right target, and in this case it is more right; the ball will have a tendency to follow the slope so it will most likely draw off this lie, curving right-to-left. So choose a target more right of where you would normally aim to accommodate for this tendency.

STEP 2

With this shot the ball is above your feet so you will need to grip down on the club. Also, the ball will not go as far with this lie, so select one more club than you normally would. Set-up to the ball by matching your spine angle with the slope and stand a bit taller. Play the ball in the upper middle of your stance.

STEP 3

Take a practice swing.

STEP 4

The key to the success of this shot is to swing with the slope. Your swing should feel flatter and more around—go with it— if you fight this, you will either dig into the slope or fall off balance and top or toe the ball.

OPTION 1:

I hit my 3-wood here for a downhill, but makeable 2-putt. In fact, I lag it close for a tap in Par!

Would you rather miss

Here...

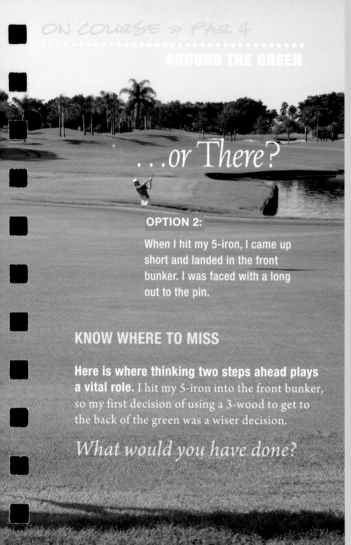

AROUND THE GREEN

…or There?

OPTION 2:

When I hit my 5-iron, I came up short and landed in the front bunker. I was faced with a long out to the pin.

KNOW WHERE TO MISS

Here is where thinking two steps ahead plays a vital role. I hit my 5-iron into the front bunker, so my first decision of using a 3-wood to get to the back of the green was a wiser decision.

What would you have done?

LOB WEDGE (60°)

SAND WEDGE (56°)

9-IRON

THE RIGHT SPOT

There is more than one way to get the ball in the hole. The key is to select the right landing area on the green. The right landing area depends on what club you choose. Be sure to look at where you do **not** want to end up. For example, landing past the hole is not optimal because you are left with a downhill, down grain putt, which is no fun.

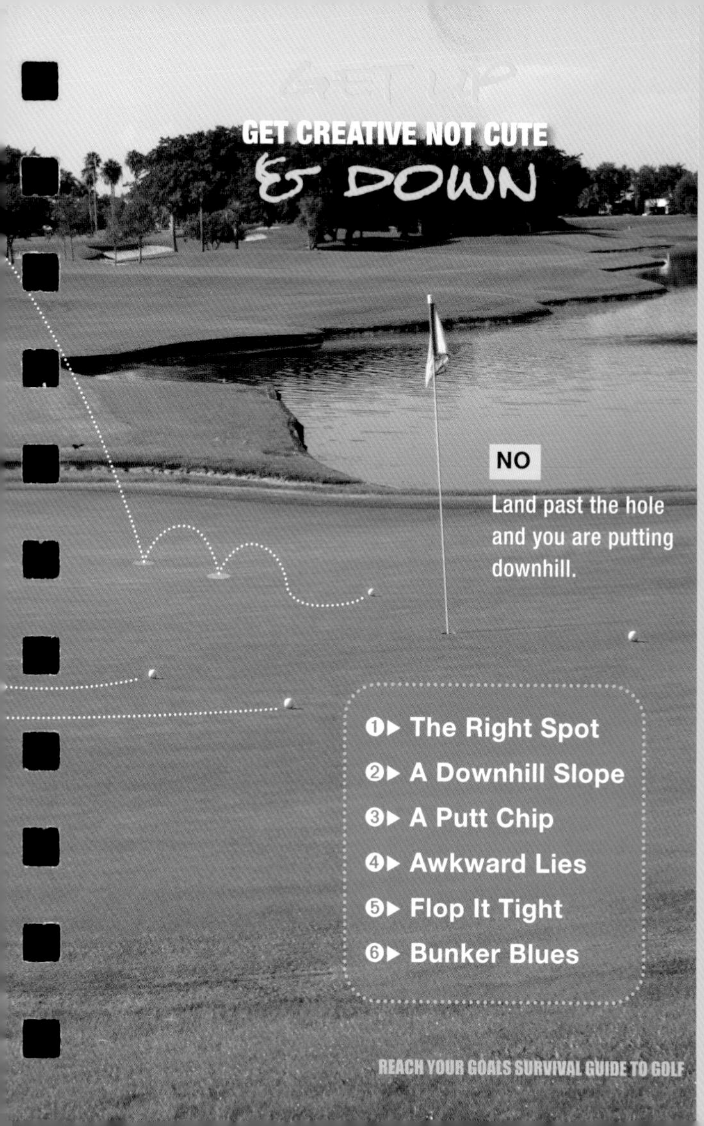

GET UP

GET CREATIVE NOT CUTE

& DOWN

NO

Land past the hole
and you are putting
downhill.

STEP 1

Choose a SW or even better a lob wedge (60°) which has more loft. Align your shoulders with the slope.

❷▶ **GET UP & DOWN**

A DOWNHILL SLOPE

A SLIPPERY DOWNHILL SLOPE

This shot is no doubt one of the toughest chips. Your objective is to create airtime with a soft landing; otherwise, this ball is going well past the hole, if not to another zip code. So here's the set-up.

STEP 2

Play the ball slightly back of center. I like a wider base to promote quiet legs.

Watch this lesson topic online!

STEP 3

With a light grip pressure make an easy backswing and downswing with zero tension. Feel like gravity is dropping the club down through impact. Because of your set-up and club selection, the ball should come out high and land soft.

Christina's **2¢**

Choose your landing area, which may be the fringe.

YES

Keep the hands low and the clubface open on the follow-through.

A PUTT CHIP

PUTT FROM A TIGHT FRINGE

This shot is a great option if your ball is close to the collar and on the fringe. Use your putter to pop the ball on to the green.

STEP 1

Set-up as you normally would for a putt and play the ball slightly back of center.

STEP 2

Your angle of attack will be steeper. Your goal is to avoid the collar and hit down on the ball.

STEP 3

On the backswing
let your wrists
hinge.

STEP 4

Keeping your hands ahead creates a descending blow. The ball should pop on to the green and roll.

STEP 1

Set yourself as best you can. Grip down on the club because the ball is above your feet. Hover the club, open the face and align your shoulders with the slope.

④▶ GET UP & DOWN
AWKWARD LIES

BALL ABOVE YOUR FEET

STEP 2

Make a
backswing with
good wrist hinge.

Pro Tip: *"The tendency is for the clubface to shut or close through impact, so open the face and make sure your grip is firm."*
- Marc Spencer

237

STEP 3

Accelerate the clubhead through the grass to your finish.

STEP 4

The clubface should still be open. Your finish will be abbreviated, simply because of the awkward stance at set-up.

HOW TO HIT FROM A DOWNSLOPE

STEP 1

Set yourself as best you can. Hover your sand or lob wedge and open the face. Align your shoulders with the slope. I like to grip down with this shot for better control.

STEP 2

Make a
backswing with
good wrist hinge.

Christina's 2¢
I like to wear my glasses with these funky shots, better safe than sorry.

STEP 4

Swing to a relaxed finish with the clubface open.

STEP 3

Swing down the slope well past impact to ensure you stay in the shot.

STEP 1

Set-up slightly left of your landing area to produce a slight out-to-in path which will produce the high, soft flight with stopping power.

Pro Tip: *"Do not forward press your shaft. Lean the shaft away from the target slightly. This set-up adds more loft, for extra stopping power."* -Marc Spencer

244

NO

Watch your alignment. It is common to see players aim too far right of the hole.

⑤► GET UP & DOWN

FLOP IT TIGHT

They say this is one of the toughest shots in golf; however, I believe everyone should have this shot in their bag. This shot requires zero tension to pull it off. If you struggle with tension in your swing, master this shot and your other short shots will be a breeze. The flop shot is very similar in feel to a sand shot, in that you want the club to slide under the ball with an open face and remain open through the finish.

YES

Your finish should be here, three-quarters.

Watch this lesson topic online!

STEP 2

Make a long and fluid backswing with good wrist hinge.

STEP 3

Your clubface remains open through the shot.

247

BUNKER BLUES

SET-UP

Make a fluid backswing.

YES

BUNKER SET-UP

STEP 1

Like the Flop shot, set-up slightly left of your landing area to produce a slight out-to-in path which will produce a high, soft flight with stopping power. Ball is positioned in the upper middle of your stance.

YES

Vary your finish to control distance.

STEP 2

Accelerate through the sand to your desired finish. I like to control the length of my bunker shot with the length of my finish and the speed of the clubhead. My backswing is the same, my finish and clubhead speed through the sand dictate the length of the shot.

Watch this lesson topic online!

BACK BUNKER

STEP 1

Position the ball in the back of your stance. Use a square clubface, with hands set slightly ahead and your weight favoring your left leg.

I get this lie more often than I should, so I have become quite comfortable with this shot. Let's get you comfortable as well. It is not difficult if you keep your focus and have a good set-up. The goal is to create a steep descent into the back of the ball, hitting the sand first, of course.

STEP 2

Make an upright and steep backswing with lots of wrist hinge.

STEP 3

Maintaining a smooth tempo, swing down the slope well past impact keeping your hands ahead. Your finish will be low and abbreviated.

STEP 4

The ball will come out low and roll more. The goal is to get the ball out and avoid the big number.

SET-UP FOR HARD SAND

STEP 1

Position the ball in the middle of your stance. Set-up with a slightly open face and hands ahead. Weight favors left leg.

Set-up with a slightly open face.

STEP 2

Make an upright and steep backswing with lots of wrist hinge. Weight still favoring left side.

STEP 3

Swing down into the sand, keeping your hands ahead. Your finish will be low and abbreviated. The ball should pop out and on to the green.

Bunker Musts
and must nots

NO

Raking your way into the bunker is against the rules. This is considered testing the sand. A 2-stroke penalty in stroke play, and loss of hole in match play.

NO

YES

257

PUTTING

A GOOD SET-UP = BETTER PUTTS

BASICS

❶▶ Loft Affects Set-up

❷▶ Be Confident

❸▶ Be Quiet

❹▶ Speed

❺▶ 1, 2, 3...It's In

❻▶ Relax

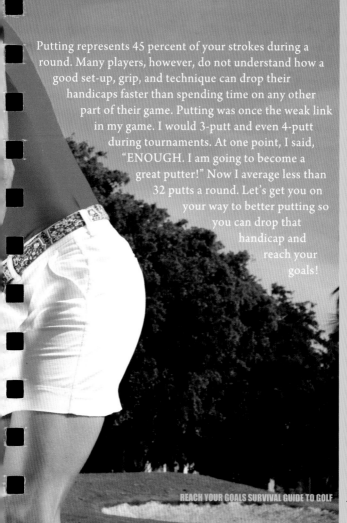

Putting represents 45 percent of your strokes during a round. Many players, however, do not understand how a good set-up, grip, and technique can drop their handicaps faster than spending time on any other part of their game. Putting was once the weak link in my game. I would 3-putt and even 4-putt during tournaments. At one point, I said, "ENOUGH. I am going to become a great putter!" Now I average less than 32 putts a round. Let's get you on your way to better putting so you can drop that handicap and reach your goals!

YES

If your putter has 2 degrees of loft, there is no need to forward press, so set your hands in line with the putter. If your putter has 3-4 degrees of loft, you can forward press.

LOFT AFFECTS SET-UP

Most putters come with 3-4 degrees of loft. Some only have 2 degrees of loft. Putters have loft because the ball does get airborne, just slightly, as it leaves the putterface. My suggestion: find out what degree of loft your putter has, so you can set-up for a successful roll in to the back of the cup.

YES

Position the ball more forward if your putter has 2 degrees of loft. If your putter has 3-4 degrees, you can position the ball as shown or in the middle of your stance.

BE CONFIDENT

Visualize
for
Success

YES

Visualize a massive hole, and sink more putts.

YES
On the short putts, keep your head quiet and listen for the drop.

Listen for the Drop

NO

Do not pick up
your head to
view the line.

YES

Do swivel your head
while maintaining your
posture to view the line.

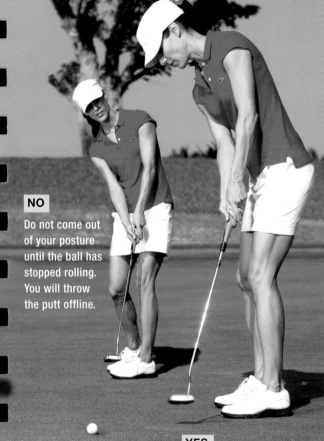

NO

Do not come out of your posture until the ball has stopped rolling. You will throw the putt offline.

YES

Do keep your body, especially your head, quiet until the ball has stopped rolling—hopefully in the hole!

265

The speed of greens varies depending on how often they are cut, and from course to course. Adjust to the speed with this pre-putt routine.

❹▶ PUTTING BASICS
Speed

YES

If you are playing greens that are slower, take your practice stroke further than your actual putt.

YES

If you are playing greens that are faster, take your practice stroke closer than your actual putt.

SHORT BACKSTROKE

For the short putts I like a short backstroke. My tempo is the same for the back and forward stroke. I make sure my putterhead releases to the hole and I hold my finish for 3 seconds.

1, 2, 3

...IT'S IN

YES

Hold your finish for 3 seconds to ensure you stay in your posture.

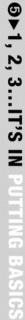

Watch this lesson topic online!

NO

A tense face, arms or
shoulders will not
provide less than 32
putts a round!

You can have the perfect grip, but if you are death-
gripping 'forgetaboutit'. Too much tension either in
your hands, arms, or shoulders will send your putt offline. Also, relax your face and lose the pursed lips. Be
aware of all parts of your body that may carry tension
and relax them. You'll make more putts with a
tension-free stroke.

YES

Relax your arms and shoulders—get comfortable.

271

YARDS: 125 TO PIN, NO. 17 HANDICAP HOLE, PIN FRONT

KNOW YOUR YARDAGES

Par 3's are not taking seriously enough. If you look back on your rounds, what was your average score on Par 3s? Many players look at a Par 3 as a breather—a shorter distance, so they take a mental break and coast. That is mental mistake number one. The second mistake, again mental, is the presence of hazards such as water. Even if you are not afraid of the water hazard, it is still a factor. For example, if I miss my 8-iron even a little, I am in the water. If I am long, I am in the back bunker. I could go for Option 2 or 3 and trust my wedge and putter?

What would you do?

OPTION 1:

An aggressive play: take dead aim at the pin with my 8-iron.

OPTION 2:

Go for the front, wide area of the green for a long putt.

OPTION 3:

Avoid the water and lay-up for a short wedge onto the green.

273

155
"If I hit it here
I am going
home."

142
125
118

ASSESS YOUR OPTIONS

I have an opportunity to make birdie here if I know
my exact yardage and commit to the right club
choice. The first step in selecting the right club is
to make sure you know how far you hit each club,
otherwise, you're playing a guessing game.

142
118
112

REACH YOUR GOALS SURVIVAL GUIDE TO GOLF

COOL IT "TIGER"

More common with men: they get too complicated when determining the ball flight. If it is a straight shot to the hole, why would you complicate it with a particular ball flight? Keep it simple!

A GOOD OPTION

If you do not have a range finder you can check the yardage the old fashioned and trusted way: with a pin sheet and yardage book.

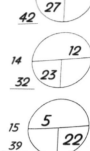

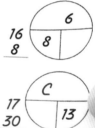

17

Green Depth
20 yards

on this hol...
...urther than it plays...
...ocus on your targe...
make a confident sw...

ar 3   Yard...
        Handi...

HOW TO
Focus on the Target
WITH A GOOD ROUTINE

STEP 1

Take your practice
swing behind the ball
looking out towards
the target.

STEP 2

Walk into the ball with your grip set, focusing all your intentions on the target.

Pro Tip: *"The tendency is for amateurs to focus on the outcome and possible failure of the shot. Instead, the focus should be on the target, and target only."*
— Marc Spencer

STEP 3

Step into the ball with your right foot aiming your clubface to your intermediate target.

STEP 4

Set your feet, hips and shoulders parallel and left of the target line which here is five feet left of the pin.

NO

Do not step into the ball from the address position and then try to aim the clubface.

STEP 5

Stay in the shot. You will find out soon enough how close you are to your target.

LEARN HOW TO VISUALIZE

Many players use their PW or SW and just hit it somewhere on the green. The key to getting the ball close is **choosing the right landing area**, then knowing how the ball will react once it hits the green. Will it hit the green and roll, and how much, or will it bounce twice and check? My choice here is Option 2, using my SW.

What would you choose?

PERFECT YOUR

LEARN HOW TO HIT IT CRISP

CHIPS & PITCHES

①▶ Visualize
②▶ Address
③▶ Connection
④▶ Your Head

OPTION 1:

An aggressive play: Use my lob wedge and hope it checks. If I am long, I'm in the water.

OPTION 2:

Use my sand wedge to the ridge and let the ball roll to the hole following the downhill slope of the green.

OPTION 3:

Play a pitching wedge, land just on the green and let the ball roll to the hole following the downhill slope. If it checks, I will be left with a tricky putt.

Have you ever approached a chip and thought, "I have no clue where this is going?" Are you afraid of chili-dipping or skulling the ball over the green into the back bunker, or worse, in the water? Let's establish a confident set-up so you can get up and down with ease.

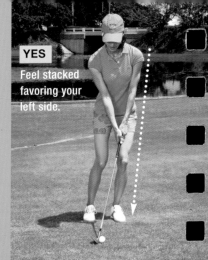

YES

Feel stacked favoring your left side.

NO

There should be no spine tilt with a chip.

NO

You will most likely scoop the ball or chunk it.

284

YES

A crisp chip. My weight is favoring my left side and staying there through the stroke.

CONNECTION

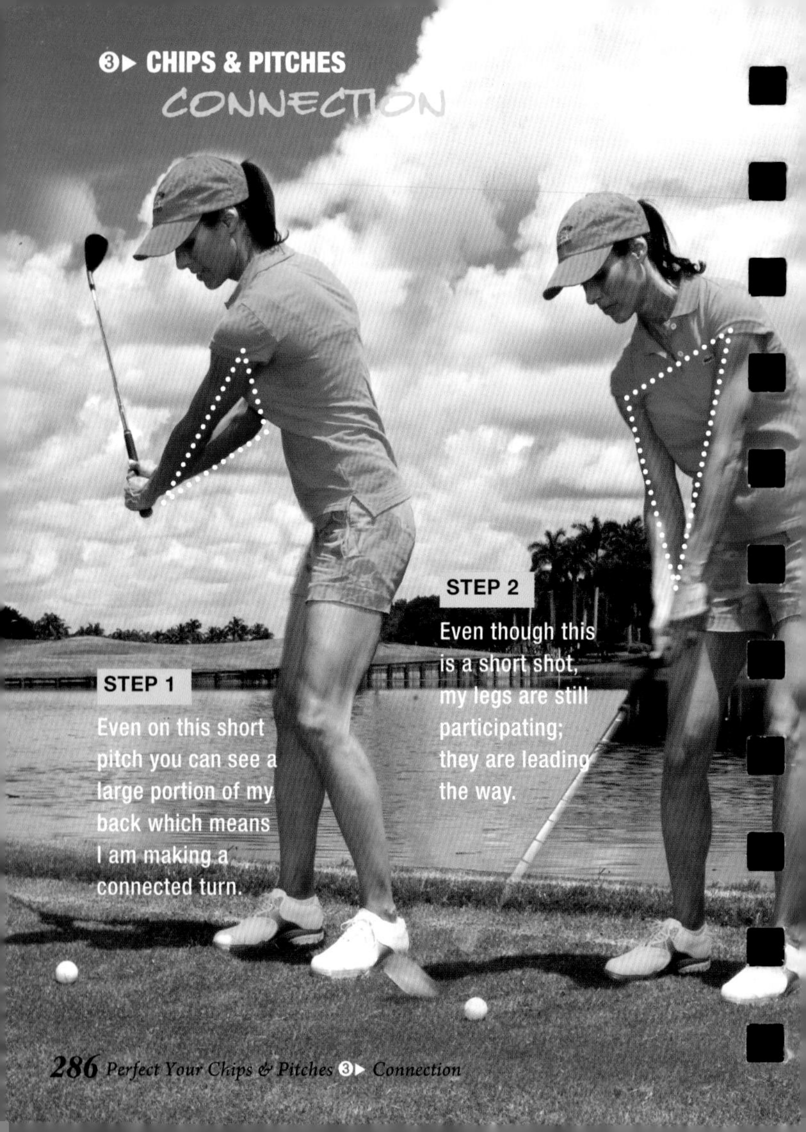

STEP 1

Even on this short pitch you can see a large portion of my back which means I am making a connected turn.

STEP 2

Even though this is a short shot, my legs are still participating; they are leading the way.

The key to pitches and chips is maintaining the connection, with your arms and shoulders working as one unit. Chicken wing releases, skulls and chunky-monkeys are a result of disconnection at some point in the swing sequence.

STEP 3

I am letting my arms release towards the target. I am not trying to guide the shot to the hole.

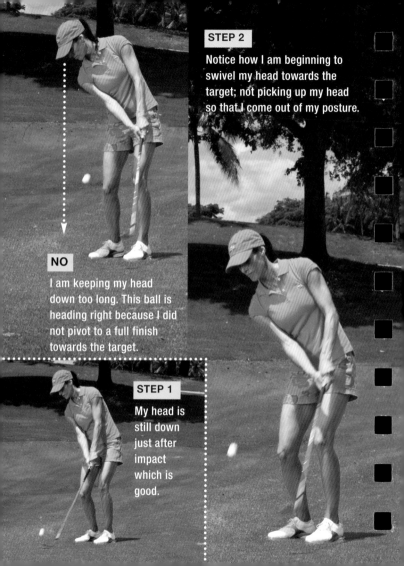

STEP 2

Notice how I am beginning to swivel my head towards the target; not picking up my head so that I come out of my posture.

NO

I am keeping my head down too long. This ball is heading right because I did not pivot to a full finish towards the target.

STEP 1

My head is still down just after impact which is good.

YOUR HEAD

KEEP IT DOWN, BUT NOT TOO LONG

We hear, "Keep your head down when hitting a chip." There is such a thing as keeping your head down too long preventing the natural pivot towards the target.

STEP 3

My head continues to swivel towards the target. My arms and shoulders are relaxed, which allows me to feel the shot. The more relaxed you are with your grip pressure, arms and shoulders, the better feel you will have to get it close.

289

I landed on the green. I pulled the shot a bit and I am left with this 40-foot putt for birdie.

NO

When tending the flag, do not allow your shadow to cross the hole.

PUTTING
BEHAVE!
ETIQUETTE

The game of golf has little tolerance for poor etiquette. Even if you are a newbie, take the time to learn the basic etiquette protocols. Your playing partners will appreciate it.

» If you are on the green and other players in your group are still chipping up, go ahead and mark your ball, it's distracting if you don't. Plus, you do not want their ball messing with yours. It is recommended to ALWAYS mark your ball.

» The person closest on the green tends the flag if needed. Be sure your shadow is not crossing the hole while tending.

YES
Always fix your divots.

» When taking the flag out, do not drop it onto the green. Place it nicely. The green is sensitive and dropping the flag haphazardly can damage the green.

» First ball in puts the flag back after everyone has putted out.

» Don't walk in anyone's line, and keep in mind this line extends three feet past the hole on that same line, in case they miss.

291

YES

It is common courtesy: the person whose ball is closest to the hole tends the flag if needed. The first person in the hole puts the flag back when everyone has putted out.

I make a good lag putt and 2-putt for Par!

Watch this lesson topic online!

NO

When taking the flag out, do not drop it onto the green. Place it nicely.

» Compliment others if they make a nice putt; however, don't say, "Nice shot." or "Nice swing." say, "Great putt!" or "You have a really nice putting stroke."

» Quiet as a mouse when a player is up—and this includes as the player is reading the putt and addressing the ball. No whispering; they can hear you, I assure you!

» Be ready to putt. Begin your pre-putt routine as you are walking towards the green. I like to check out the slope and lay of the land as I am driving up to the hole. From a further vantage point, I can clearly see how my ball will break towards the hole. It's a great technique; try it.

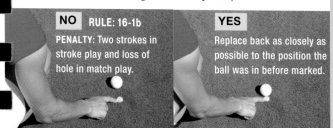

NO RULE: 16-1b
PENALTY: Two strokes in stroke play and loss of hole in match play.

YES
Replace back as closely as possible to the position the ball was in before marked.

293

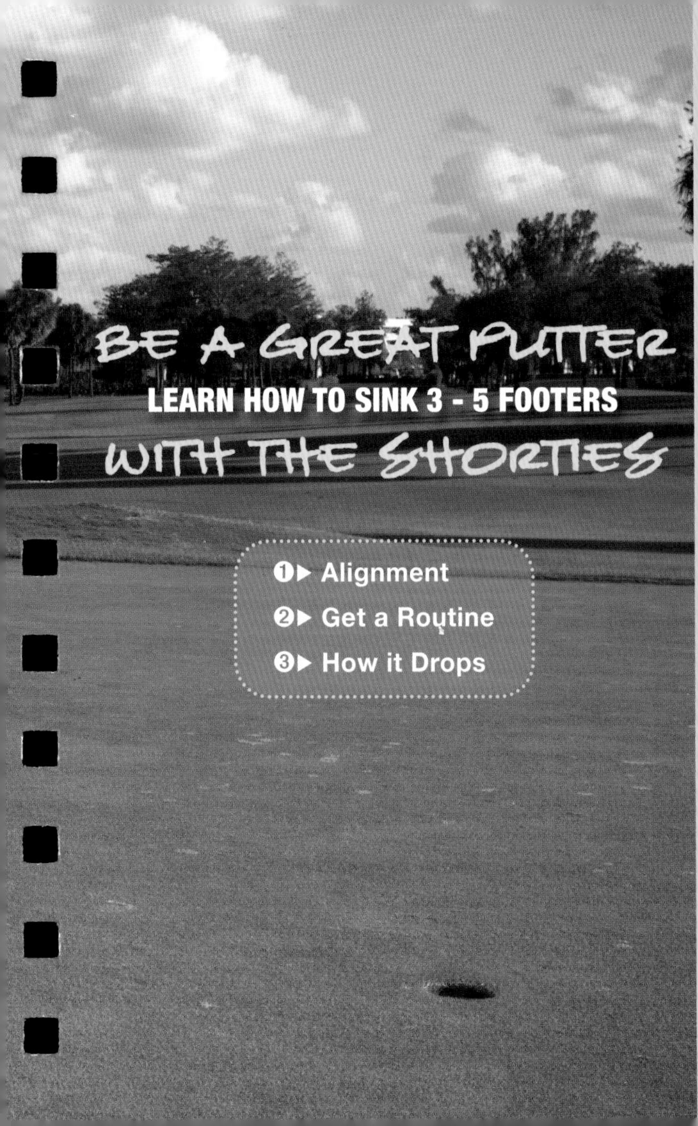

BE A GREAT PUTTER

LEARN HOW TO SINK 3 - 5 FOOTERS

WITH THE SHORTIES

❶▶ Alignment
❷▶ Get a Routine
❸▶ How it Drops

Q.

What Happened?

A. Poor Alignment.

Set the putterface square to your target.
Remember, the target may not be the
hole, but your intermediate target.

STEP 1

Always pick a spot just at
the hole where you want
the ball to roll over into
the cup.

STEP 2

Then pick a spot an inch
or so in front of the ball,
that is inline with your
main target, to set the
putterface.

Watch this lesson
topic online!

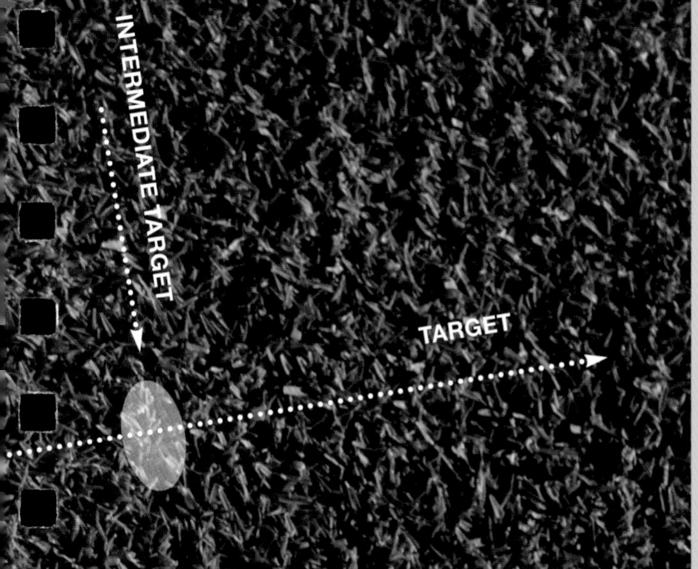

INTERMEDIATE TARGET

TARGET

YES

Use the alignment aid on the ball and the putter for perfect alignment. Set the line on your putter with the line on the ball. The line on the ball is inline with your intermediate target—foolproof putting.

Christina's **2¢**

If your putter does not have an alignment aid, then draw one on. I did.

NO
Notice how the line on the ball does not match the target line.

YES

This putt breaks right-to-left. It is a slight downhill and down grain putt. My goal is to drop the ball into the front edge of the hole. Also, notice how my putter's line matches the ball's alignment aid.

STEP 1

Align the ball to an intermediate target. Use the alignment aid on the ball.

②▶ THE SHORTIES

GET A ROUTINE

STEP 3

Take a couple of strokes to feel the speed.

STEP 2

Align the putterface to your intermediate target. Use the alignment aid on your putter to align with the alignment aid on the ball.

STEP 4

Take one last look at your intermediate target and the hole, seeing in your mind's eye, the ball dropping in the hole.

STEP 5

Stroke it in.

How do you like it to drop?

Do you prefer to die the ball in the hole like Annika, or jam it to the back of the cup like Phil? Determine your style and keep it consistent on every green and with every round.

Do you prefer to die the ball in?

Do you prefer to jam the ball to the back of the cup?

STEP 6
PRACTICE & DRILLS
PRACTICE DEFINED

PRACTICE TIME...MAKE TIME

The most overlooked element of improvement is practice. I know you are saying, "I practice." Sure you do, but how do you define practice? Success in your golf game has a direct correlation with how you approach the game and that includes on the range and around the practice green. Here are a few practice habits to adopt into your regime.

Time Allocations: It is not quantity, it's quality

Always have a plan when you head out to practice. Allocate a certain amount of time for each part of your game. It is best to focus on your weaknesses more than your strengths. In other words, focus on what you are struggling with out on the course, not the shots you have executed well.

I have 2 hours: 30 minutes putting /30 chips and pitches/ 20 bunker /40 hitting balls
I have 1 hour: 15 putting /15 chips /30 hitting balls
I have 1/2 hour: 15 putting /15 hitting balls

Are you seeing a pattern here? Spend at least 50 percent on short game—always!

Practice with a specific focus EVERY TIME you practice; otherwise, it is not practice.

Here is the scenario: Susan and Bill are at the range. I asked Susan

Set-up an alignment station when practicing.
Set a club parallel to target line to ensure accurate alignment. Next, set a club perpendicular to this club for precise ball position.

what she was working on and she said, "I am working on alignment." I said, "Great, so why don't you try this: set-up an alignment station so you can ensure your alignment is spot-on and not a guessing game. Set a club parallel to the target line and set another for ball position which would lay perpendicular to your target line. Hit a half a bucket and then take the clubs away. Hit to the same target to check your alignment."

Visualize when on the range. For example, pick a target as you would on the golf course. Visualize the ball starting just right of the red flag and drawing so it lands at the second mound behind the red flag about 50 yards. Visualizing shots on the range will help you visualize better on the course.

Pro Tip: *"Going to the driving range without a purpose is good exercise. You'll get sun, some fresh air, and maybe let off a little steam from the day. Going to the driving range with a purpose is called practice."* - Marc Spencer

ON THE GREEN
PUTTING DRILLS
PAGE 348

DRILLS ARE
LOVE DRILLS AND GET BETTER
FUN!

ON THE RANGE

❶▶ Attitude Adjustment

❷▶ Get Rid of Tension

❸▶ Fix Swing Paths

❹▶ Stop Casting

❺▶ Get Leg Drive

❻▶ Extend Yourself

❼▶ Check Your Face

❽▶ Feel Connected

❾▶ Better Impact

❿▶ Learn Feel

ATTITUDE ADJUSTMENT

"I was a bundle of overactive head movement. Fifteen minutes with the Penny Drill and I am smiling."

Drills work when they are FUN:

If you approach drills as a chore or something that you HAVE to do, then chances are, you will not enjoy yourself, or you will most likely not do them at all. Practicing with a positive attitude while having fun is the name of the game. Practice with your buddies. Have contests! It will be well worth the effort, especially, when it equates to lower scores and fewer 3-putts!

GET RID OF TENSION

THROW THE CLUB

STEP 1

Get into your normal address position, with or without a ball.

NO

If the club goes left or way behind you, you are holding on for dear life.

Many tighten their grip through the hitting area. I was one of those people. This is a great drill to test and fix your grip tension levels or any other tension in your body, for that matter. If your club goes left or behind, you have tension. Loosen up your grip pressure until you can throw the club to the target. Use that grip pressure when you set-up to your normal shot and maintain it through the finish.

STEP 2

Throw the club towards the target. Your goal is to get the club to the target.

TO CORRECT AN OUT-TO-IN SWING PATH

NO

If you hit the tee on the downswing, your path is too outside.

STEP 1

Tee your ball. Then set
a second tee as shown.

③▶ ON THE RANGE

FIX SWING PATHS

If you struggle with an over-the-top move which
typically will create a left-to-right ball flight — 'slice',
then try this tee drill to groove a better swing path.
Ideally, you would like a path that comes from the
inside producing a right-to-left ball flight, unless
you are intentionally trying to fade the ball.

317

STEP 2

Your objective is to make a swing without coming into contact with the second tee.

"Practice as if you are playing and play as if you are practicing. That way you are always practicing with a purpose and when you play, you are not putting too much pressure on yourself."

-Karen Palacios-Jansen
2008 LPGA National Teacher of the Year

YES

Make sure you leave enough room away from the teed ball for the driver to clear. Test this by making a mock inside-to-out swing path to ensure the tee is in the proper position.

Christina's **24**

A good drill to learn how to draw the ball!

STEP 1

Set two tees in the ground as shown, creating two goal posts. Tee your ball in the center of the two tees.

TWO TEE GOALIE DRILL

STEP 2

Strike the ball without hitting the two teed goal posts. If you do strike one of the tees, your path is either too outside or you may be pulling across the target line, which typically, will create a duck hook or pull.

HEAD COVER DRILL

STEP 1

Place your driver head cover outside and parallel of your teed ball.

STEP 2

Your objective is to swing on an inside path and miss the head cover through the hitting area.

NO

If you do strike the head cover, your path is either coming too outside or pulling across the target line which typically will create a duck hook or pull.

STEP 1

Set up as you normally would. You can use any club. I am using a 3-wood.

❹▶ ON THE RANGE

STOP CASTING

Plus, learn how to draw. And not with a pencil. An exaggerated draw stance: address the ball as you normally would, then pull your right foot back about eight inches. This set-up makes it very difficult to throw the club as it forces you to come from the inside while maintaining good angles. Works like a charm—try it!

STEP 2

Drop your right foot back so your right toe is inline with your left heel.

YES

Setting up with an exaggerated stance forces the club to come from a slight inside path relative to your target line. If successful, you should create a slight right-to-left ball flight. Once you master this drill, reset your stance in its normal position.

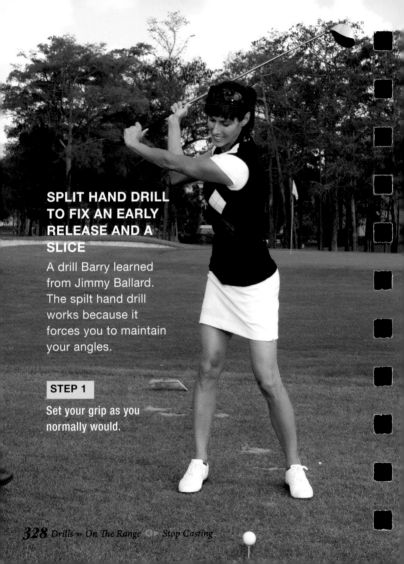

SPLIT HAND DRILL TO FIX AN EARLY RELEASE AND A SLICE

A drill Barry learned from Jimmy Ballard. The spilt hand drill works because it forces you to maintain your angles.

STEP 1

Set your grip as you normally would.

STEP 2

Slide the right hand down the grip to create a split between the hands.

STEP 3

Make a half swing at half speed and notice how this drill encourages your right hand to pass the left through impact. Notice how your forearms will rotate naturally without forcing a rotation.

329

STEP 1

Place a club inline with a teed ball.
Set your body with your feet together
on the right side of the shaft.

STEP 2

Swing to the top, start
with a half backswing.

GET LEG DRIVE

LEARN HOW TO USE YOUR LEGS

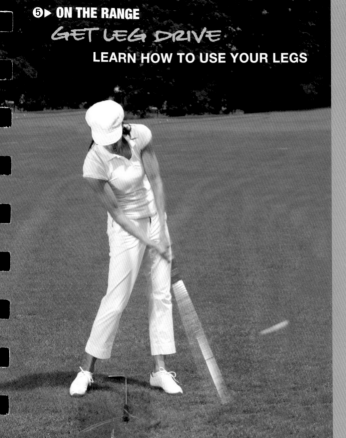

STEP 3

Initiate your downswing by stepping your left foot over the shaft, firmly planting into the turf.

STEP 4

You will be set in your normal swing position through impact.

⑥▶ ON THE RANGE

EXTEND YOURSELF

**SET-UP TO THE FIRST TEE,
HIT THE SECOND**

STEP 1

Place two tees about an iron clubhead apart.
Set your clubface to the inside 'empty' tee.
Your objective is to strike the teed ball.

A great drill to feel extension. I learned this drill while attending a three day golf school.

YES

Inside tee still intact.

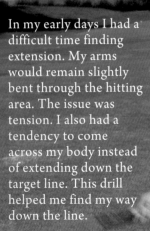

In my early days I had a difficult time finding extension. My arms would remain slightly bent through the hitting area. The issue was tension. I also had a tendency to come across my body instead of extending down the target line. This drill helped me find my way down the line.

CLIP THE SECOND TEE

STEP 1

Tee up a ball. Then place a second tee on the target line about six inches in front of the teed ball along the target line.

STEP 2

Your objective is to hit the ball, and clip the second.

YES

If you miss the second tee, check your swing path. Also, relax your arms through the impact zone. You are most likely pulling up through impact, which through experience, is typically tension in the hands, arms or shoulders.

STAY ON TARGET WITH YOUR WEDGES

STEP 1

Tee your ball. Then place a shaft on your target line about one foot away from your teed ball. I like to place a tee in front of the shaft as well.

STEP 2

Your objective is to extend your arms down the target line for as long as you can.

I see many players, and I was one of them, cut across their body (pull the club left) through impact. You not only lose your extension, your ball will not make solid contact with the clubface, and you will most likely scoop or pull the ball left of your target line. Try this drill to stay on target.

STEP 1

Ask for clubface tape at your local golf shop. Place the tape exactly as shown here. The tape will indicate toe and heel placement.

7▶ ON THE RANGE

CHECK YOUR FACE

DRILL FOR SWING AND EQUIPMENT

STEP 2

Set-up to the ball as you normally would and make a swing.

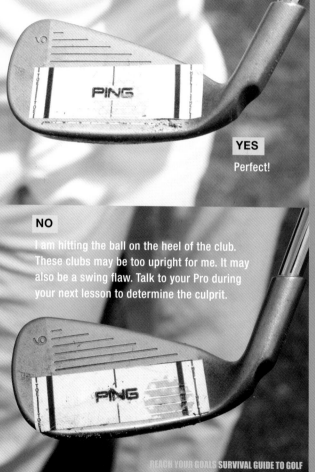

YES

Perfect!

NO

I am hitting the ball on the heel of the club.
These clubs may be too upright for me. It may
also be a swing flaw. Talk to your Pro during
your next lesson to determine the culprit.

FEEL CONNECTED

DRILL FOR BACK AND DOWNSWING

STEP 1

Place a towel under both arms and hold in place. You should feel a strong connection with your arms and chest.

STEP 2

Make a half backswing. The towel should remain intact as it was at address.

YES

Notice how the towel looks identical to my address position, firmly in place.

STEP 3

Make your normal swing to a complete finish.

341

Christina's 2¢

🌱 The Towel Drill is one of my faves. It ingrains the feeling of a good connection.

NO

If you lose the towel in any part of your half-swing then check your arms. They are moving away from your upper body.

NO

You are most likely
lifting your arms
instead of making
a shoulder turn.
Your arms and
shoulders should
act as one unit.

STEP 1
The Impact Ball is placed between your forearms.

STEP 2
Start with chip shots.

⑨► ON THE RANGE
BETTER IMPACT

A great drill to teach how to hit down with your hands leading. Also a great drill to teach how to maintain the triangle created by your hands, arms and shoulders—a must for solid, crisp chips! Use the Impact Ball for your 50-75 yard wedge shots too.

STEP 3

Maintain the Impact Ball through the chip. If it falls, you allowed your angles to breakdown.

NO

My hand finished too high.

STEP 1

Stand about 30 yards from the flag with a ball in hand.

STEP 2

Toss the ball onto the green. Your objective is to get it close to the flag, simulating a chip shot.

YES

I discovered when I kept my
hand low through the toss, I
had better distance control.
It's the same deal with a club.

10 ▶ ON THE RANGE

LEARN FEEL

TOSS THE BALL

TOSS THE BALL DRILL

Many say you cannot teach feel. I disagree. I was
told I had no feel around the green. I never
listened to a word of it because I knew I had feel.
It was just trapped inside a tense body.

A great way to rediscover your feel is to toss a
ball with a friend. Stand six feet apart then move
further away with each toss. Your objective is to
create a high, soft toss, not a low screamer. The
second drill shown here, will not only teach you
feel, but distance control around the green.

ON THE
DRILLS FOR PRACTICE
GREEN

"I don't need to practice putting."

For those who believe that practicing their putting is a waste of time, I would like to challenge you to putting practice for one week, fifteen minutes a day. I guarantee you will see more putts drop out on the course. I am sure you agree that the long game and shots around the green require solid technique, good alignment and feel, so why wouldn't putting? Good putting is not acquired in your sleep. For those who see drills as a chore, here are some easy and fun drills to get you putting your best and averaging 32 putts or less a round. Wouldn't that be nice?

ON THE GREEN

❶▶ Black Stripes

❷▶ Two Tees

❸▶ Touchdown

❹▶ Got Penny?

❺▶ 8 Feet and In

❻▶ Around the World

❼▶ Take the High Road

❽▶ Got Wrist?

❾▶ Tennis Ball Drill

❿▶ Positively Positive

BLACK STRIPES

Drill to Find the Perfect Roll

A great drill to help you make solid contact using a range ball like the one shown below. You need a ball that has heavy lines. If you do not have this type at your club, go ahead and add one or two thick lines to your ball.

NO

Notice how the lines on the ball are wobbling, not perpendicular to the green, but slanted.

STEP 1

Set-up to the ball as you normally would.

STEP 2

Make a stroke. Your objective is to roll the ball so the lines become one.

YES

Notice how the lines on the ball are perpendicular to the green, rolling with the lines straight up and down.

STEP 1

Place two tees in the ground at a width slightly wider than your putter.

ADVANCED:
Place the tees barely wider than your putter.

STEP 2

Make your normal putting stroke. If you hit one of the tees on your forward stroke, check your swing path.

②▶ ON THE GREEN

TWO TEES

A Good Drill for Swing Path

A simple drill you can do every time you practice putting or as a pre-tee-off warm-up. This drill forces you to make solid contact. If you graze the tees during your stroke, it means you are either too inside or too outside on your path. Also, you may be too wristy.

TOUCHDOWN

A Good Drill for Swing Path and Alignment

The Anatomy of a Good Putt ············▶

How to do it: Place two tees about half-way to the hole on the intended line. Your objective is to putt your ball through the tees. This drill helps you pick the correct line and ensures your alignment is spot-on. Make certain to set the drill up so that if the ball rolls through the two tees at the right speed, it will go in the hole.

Watch any great putter, like Kevin. Notice his head; he keeps it down well after he has stroked the putt. Copy this and do it always. Your putting will improve.

357

GOT PENNY?

A Good Drill for an Overactive Head

NO

I peeked!

The Anatomy of a Not-So-Good Putt

As you can see, my head came up just as I stroked the putt. It moved the ball offline, typically a miss left of the hole.

A great drill to fix an active head. You can do this drill every time you practice putting, or as a pre-tee-off warm-up drill.

YES

Notice how my head stays quiet well after the ball leaves the putterface.

How to do it: Place a penny on the ground and determine if the penny is tails up or heads up immediately after you stroke the putt.

⑤▸ ON THE GREEN

8 Feet & In

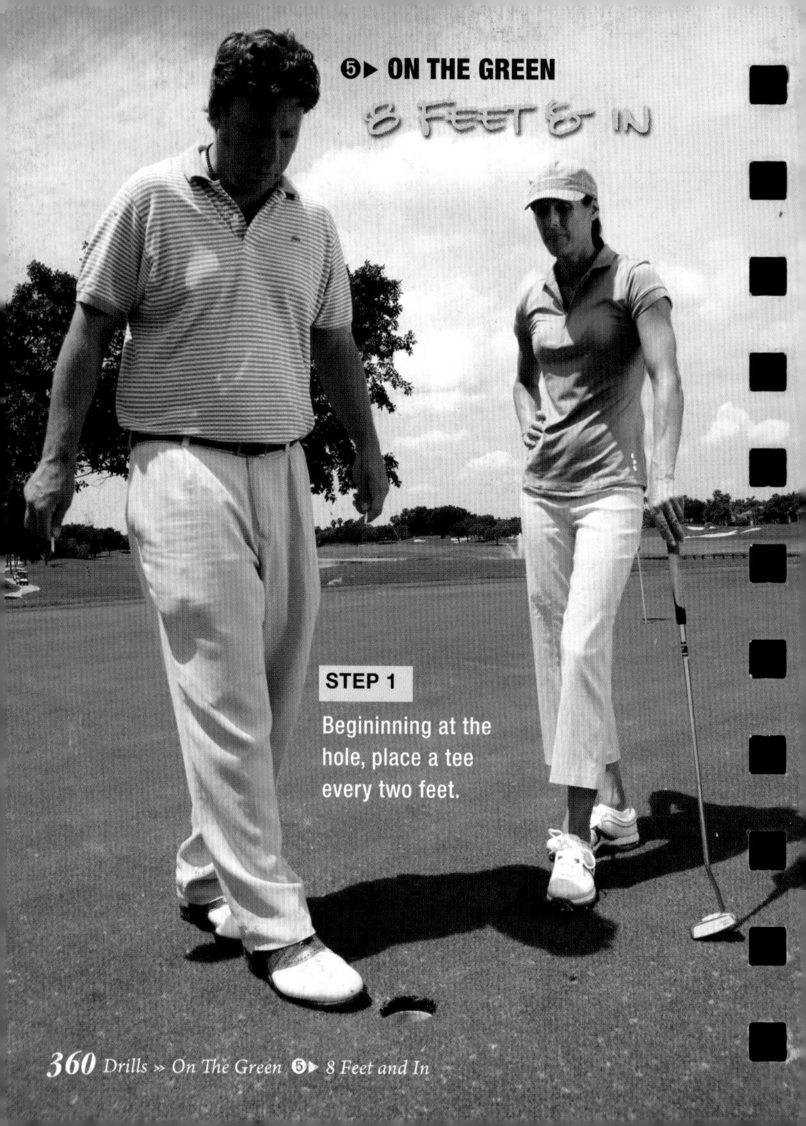

STEP 1

Begininning at the hole, place a tee every two feet.

YES

Place the tee at your heel.

MASTER THE 8 AND INS

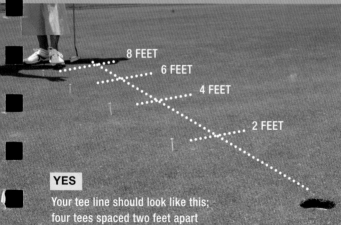

8 FEET

6 FEET

4 FEET

2 FEET

YES

Your tee line should look like this;
four tees spaced two feet apart
forming a line.

STEP 2

Your objective is to putt a total of 12 balls consecutively into the hole, beginning with the tee closest to the hole. So putt 3 balls from 2 feet, 3 balls from 4 feet etc.

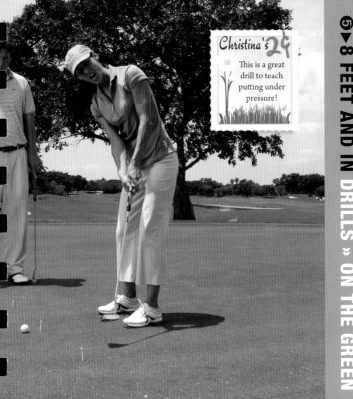

Christina's 2¢

This is a great drill to teach putting under pressure!

STEP 3

If you miss a putt, you start over from tee number one.

AROUND THE WORLD

Be a better putter from 4 feet and in

STEP 1

Place 4 tees, 4 feet from the hole on all 4 quadrants.

IMPROVE YOUR CONFIDENCE

This is a great drill to improve your confidence with short putts, but also line. Placing the tees on all four quadrants forces you to consider the line as well as the speed. To make this drill tougher, choose a hole that has some undulation, so you can learn to make those four footers from anywhere.

STEP 2

Your objective is to
putt a total of 12
balls consecutively
into the hole—putt 3
from each quadrant.

STEP 1

Select a breaking putt and place a tee just inside the apex of the line.

❼▶ ON THE GREEN

TAKE THE HIGH ROAD

Learn to Miss on the 'Pro Side'

This is a great drill to improve your read on breaking putts. Your goal is to miss on the high side of the cup, also known as the 'Pro Side' of the cup.

"Ninety percent of missed putts are missed on the 'low side', meaning players do not play enough break."

- Marc Spencer

STEP 2

Walk into the putt from behind the ball, not the side.

NO

STEP 3

Set your putterface to an intermediate target a few inches ahead on the target line.

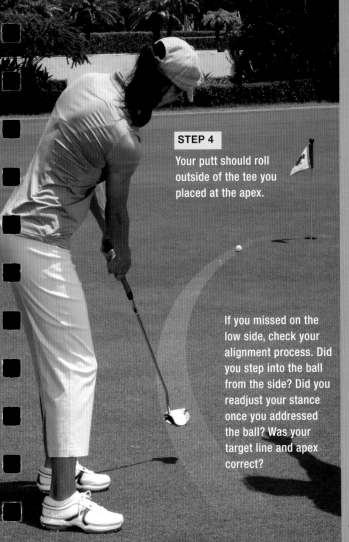

STEP 4

Your putt should roll outside of the tee you placed at the apex.

If you missed on the low side, check your alignment process. Did you step into the ball from the side? Did you readjust your stance once you addressed the ball? Was your target line and apex correct?

NO

A cupped wrist through impact will not produce solid putts.

⑧▶ ON THE GREEN

GOT WRIST?

Fix a wristy and scoopy stroke with Drill No. 8 and 9

STEP 1

Set your left hand at the top half of the shaft, then slide your right hand down the shaft close to the end of the grip, as shown.

YES

STEP 2

Make your normal stroke. You should feel like your hands, arms and shoulders are working as one unit. A great drill to fix a wristy stroke.

371

TENNIS BALL DRILL

Take your wrists out of the equation

STEP 1

Place a tennis ball between your wrists. If you are practicing with a buddy, have him place the ball between your wrists, I found this to be easier.

STEP 2

Make your normal stroke. If the ball falls out, you are using your wrists.

This is a great drill to eliminate a wristy putting stroke. I learned this drill from PGA Professional and Author of *Golf, The Ultimate Mind Game*, Rick Sessinghaus. By placing a tennis ball between your wrists, you are forced to make a stroke using your shoulders, arms and hands as one unit.

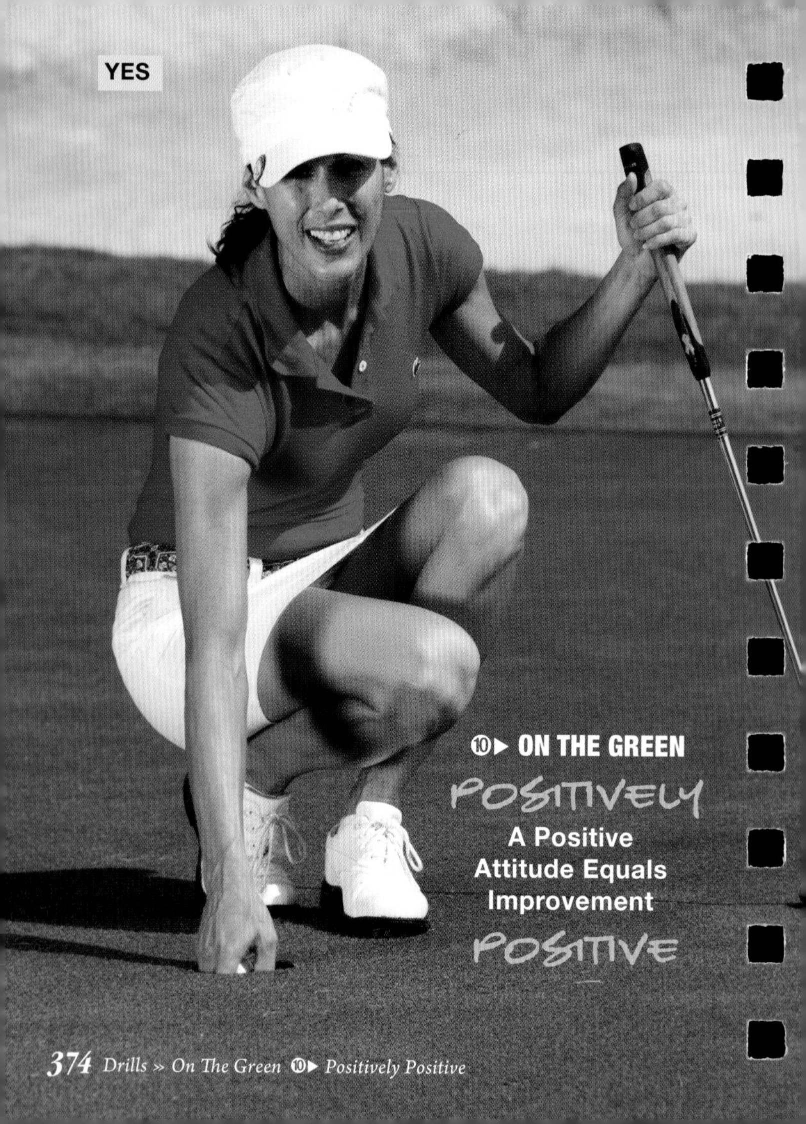

YES

10 ▶ ON THE GREEN

POSITIVELY

A Positive
Attitude Equals
Improvement

POSITIVE

NO

If you are practicing a drill and cannot seem to master the drill, be patient. Good things come to those who are patient and open to change. If you practice, but are continually making the same errors because you feel change is uncomfortable, then get in line. Most of us resist change, at first. If you embrace new feelings and sensations, even if it feels awkward, you will be two steps ahead of the pack and on your way to reaching your goals this season.

STEP 7
THE SUPER BASICS
RULES & ETIQUETTE

Rules are your friend most of the time,

especially when it comes to knowing your options. If you find your ball in a hazard, do you know that you have options? Let's examine these options so the next time you find yourself wayward, you can make an educated decision to save Par.

What's at Stake?

RULE 26: DO YOU KNOW YOUR WHITE, YELLOW AND REDS?

WHITE STAKES AND WHITE LINES

White stakes or white lines are used to indicate out-of-bounds. A course can mark out-of-bounds in other ways too; for example, a fence might mark the boundary along certain parts of a course. If you hit your ball out-of-bounds assess yourself a 1-stroke penalty, return to the spot of the previous shot and hit it again; a stroke-and-distance penalty. To maintain pace of play, if a player believes his ball may be OB, it is suggested to hit a provisional ball.

YELLOW STAKES AND YELLOW LINES

Yellow stakes and lines indicate a water hazard.

If a ball crosses the margin of a water hazard (designated by the yellow stakes or yellow lines), but is not actually in water, it might be easily playable. If a ball is under water; however, it's almost always best to take the penalty and put a new ball into play.

You have 3 options for YELLOW stakes

OPTION 1: Play it as it lies, no penalty.

OPTION 2: Return to the spot from where the previous stroke was played and play it again, 'stroke and distance'.

OPTION 3: You can take a drop. The drop can be made at any point, as far back as you wish, as long as the point where the ball crossed into the hazard is kept between the point of the drop and the hole. In other words, keep the point from where the ball last crossed the margin of the hazard and go back as far as you want keeping that point between you and the flagstick.

WHEN IS A BALL IN A HAZARD?

A ball is considered in the hazard when it lies within the hazard or when any part of it touches the hazard; that includes stakes and lines, which are part of the hazard.

Know
your
options

**RULE 26
LATERAL HAZARD,
RED STAKES OR
RED LINES**

Play the ball
from where it
lies with no
penalty.

YOU HAVE 5 OPTIONS FOR RED STAKES

Option 1: Play it as it lies, no penalty.

Option 2: You may drop within two club-lengths of the point of entry, but no nearer the hole—a 1-stroke penalty.

Option 3: Drop behind the hazard on a line formed by the hole and the point where the ball entered the hazard—a 1-stroke penalty.

Option 4: A player can go to the opposite side of the hazard and drop at a spot on the hazard's margin that is equidistant from the hole—a 1-stroke penalty.

Option 5: You may return to the tee or the last spot from which you played the ball. So, in the hazard on 1, out in 2, hitting 3.

RED STAKES AND RED LINES

Red stakes and lines indicate a lateral water hazard. A lateral water hazard is differentiated from a water hazard as its name implies because it is lateral. It runs alongside the line of play, rather than across it.

Option 2

A player can assess themselves a 1-stroke penalty and take a drop.

STEP 1

Place a tee as close as possible to where your original ball went into the hazard.

NO

You are not allowed to ground your club in a hazard or you will incur a 2-stroke penalty in stroke play and loss of hole in match play.

How to execute Option 2: The drop can be taken within two club lengths from the point where the ball crossed the margin of the hazard, no nearer the hole.

Using your longest club, measure two club lengths beginning at where you placed the tee.

STEP 3

Place a tee at the second club length and put your club away.

STEP 4

Standing within the two club lengths, hold your arm parallel to the ground and drop the ball.

WHEN TO REDROP

A dropped ball must be redropped without penalty in this situation, if it (a) rolls into and comes to rest back in the hazard; (b) rolls out of and comes to rest more than two club lengths from where it first went into the hazard; or (c) comes to rest closer to the hole. If this occurs, then a player can place the ball as near as possible to the spot where it landed on the second drop.

WHO DROPS, AND HOW

A ball to be dropped under the Rules must be dropped by the player himself. He must stand erect, hold the ball at shoulder height and arm's length and drop it. If a ball is dropped by any other person or in any other manner and the error is not corrected as provided in Rule 20-6, the player incurs a penalty of one stroke.

NO

Rule 20-2 the act of flicking, tossing or manipulating the drop in any way incurs a 1-stroke penalty.

Option 3

You can assess yourself a 1-stroke penalty and take a drop behind the hazard. You can go as far back as you want, but you MUST maintain a straight line between three points: the hole, where your ball originally entered the hazard, and you.

Option 4

You can assess yourself a 1-stroke penalty and take a drop on the opposite side and equidistant from where the ball first crossed into the hazard. Once there, you drop within two club lengths from the hazard, as explained in Option 2.

Option 5

You can assess yourself a 1-stroke penalty and return to the tee or the last spot from which you last played the ball—hitting three.

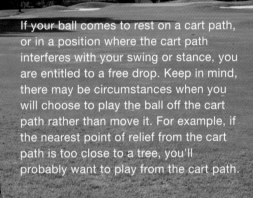

If your ball comes to rest on a cart path, or in a position where the cart path interferes with your swing or stance, you are entitled to a free drop. Keep in mind, there may be circumstances when you will choose to play the ball off the cart path rather than move it. For example, if the nearest point of relief from the cart path is too close to a tree, you'll probably want to play from the cart path.

Cart Path CAN I MOVE IT?

RULE 24-2: IMMOVABLE OBSTRUCTION

STEP 1

Place a tee next to your ball then lift it.

STEP 2

Using your longest club measure one club length from the tee, no nearer to the hole.

STEP 3

Stand with arms outreached and parallel to the ground. Drop within the one club length.

KEEP YOUR FRIENDS
TEE TO GREEN: GOOD STUFF TO KNOW
AND MAKE NEW ONES

"No zippers, no yip-yapping including the slightest whisper!"

GENERAL

☞ When someone is preparing to hit the ball, stay out of his peripheral vision.

☞ When a player is up and begins her routine—which starts the moment she takes the club out of the bag—be quiet! This means: no zippers, club noise, no yip-yapping, including the slightest whisper. She can hear you—I assure you!

ON THE TEE BOX

☞ Never tee-it-up in front of the tee box markers or you will incur a 2-stroke penalty in stroke play (shown next page).

☞ Be ready to hit—don't be searching for tees or dilly-dallying on club selection. Instead, prep a shot while others are hitting, so when it's your turn you are ready to roll—this is called pace of play.

☞ If your tee shot is hit out of bounds or potentially out of bounds, hit a provisional—again pace of play.

IN THE FAIRWAY

☞ Know the cart rules for the day. Is it 90 degrees, cart path only?

☞ The ball furthest from the hole is played first.

☞ Don't drive, talk or walk in front of a player while she is preparing to hit her shot—this is super-rude, and, not to mention, dangerous!

☞ Help a player find his ball if he hits it in the woods, rough, or similar 'unpretty' spot.

☞ If you find yourself with an 'unpretty lie, don't even think about improving it— it's against the rules.

Cont'd page 394 ☞

Where to Tee It

NO

Never tee-it-up in front of the tee box markers or you'll incur a 2-stroke penalty in stroke play.

A pair of tee markers defines the boundaries of the teeing ground. The front, left and right sides of the tee are denoted by the outer edges of the tee markers, assuming the perspective of a player standing in the teeing ground and facing the hole. The teeing ground is two club-lengths in depth. On the tee box, you must place your ball between the tee markers, either even with them or up to two club lengths behind them. Never in front of them.

YES

Always tee-it-up behind the tee box markers.

"Leave your ego at the clubhouse. Play the appropriate tees suited to your game!"

👉 Compliment someone if they hit a nice shot; however, don't do it for every shot, just the really good ones, or ones you know they were worried about making. Make sure the outcome was actually good. Don't say it for the sake of it, or to kiss you-know-what. Sincerity, my friend—sincerity rules!

👉 If you find yourself in a lateral hazard, you do have the option of hitting, but remember, do not ground your club— it's against the rules.

👉 If you are playing a Par 4 and you are hitting your eighth shot, and still have 200 yards from the hole, pick-up. If you are with buddies, just drop somewhere near the green so you can at least hole out, but only if you are with buddies, and not if it's a competition of any kind. Give yourself a max score for the hole. So if a Par 4, take an 8.

AROUND THE GREEN

☞ Never drive the cart or place your bag or hand cart on the green.

☞ If your ball lands in a bunker, step into the bunker on the low side to avoid damaging the bunker by stepping down a steep incline.

☞ Never rake the bunker as your enter. Further, rake the bunker with a rake, not your club! » Page 257

☞ Never ground your club in a bunker.

☞ You are not allowed to move loose impediments in a bunker: a rock, leaf or branch.

ON THE GREEN Behave on the putting surface » Page 290

Marc Spencer (left) and Mario Muñoz (right) with me at Weston Hills Country Club in Weston, Florida

ACKNOWLEDGEMENTS

ACKNOWLEDGEMENTS I would like to thank PGA professionals: Kevin Sprecher, the Director of Instruction at the Sleepy Hollow C.C., NY (www.kevinsprecher.com); Barry Goldstein of Inverrary Country Club in Fort Lauderdale, FL; and Marc Spencer of the Atkinson Resort and Country Club, NH (atkinsonresort.com), for sharing their Pro-wisdom in this Guide. I would like to thank Mike Blazer for providing access to a wonderful golf course, Weston Hills C.C., FL; Mario Muñoz for taking spectacular photographs; Richard, my mother's perpetual fiancé, for introducing me to this wonderful world of golf; and lastly, I would like to extend a special thanks to Robert Kraut, and the Booklegger family for all their support.